100 Things Every
Writer Needs to Know

Scott Edelstein

A Perigee Book

Most Perigee Books are available at special quantity discounts for bulk purchases for sales promotions, premiums, fund-raising or educational use. Special books, or book excerpts, can also be created to fit specific needs.

For details, write: Special Markets: The Berkley Publishing Group, 375 Hudson Street, New York, New York 10014.

ACKNOWLEDGMENTS

The sample netlines on pages 49–51 are reprinted from the following sources:

Page 49: *Surviving Freshman Composition.* © 1988 by Scott Edelstein. Published by arrangement with Carol Publishing Group.

Page 50: *30 Steps to Becoming a Writer—and Getting Published.* © 1993 by Scott Edelstein. Published by arrangement with F&W Publications.

Page 51: *The No-Experience-Necessary Writer's Course.* © 1990 by Scott Edelstein. Published by arrangement with Scarborough House and National Book Network.

The sample manuscript pages and sample letters on pages 141–146, the sample assignment agreement on page 147, and the sample letter to agents on page 193 originally appeared, in somewhat different form, in *The Indispensable Writer's Guide* (HarperCollins). © 1989 by Scott Edelstein.

The sample letter to agents on page 193 also appears here by permission of Mary Kuhfeld.

The sample letter to agents on page 194 appears here by permission of Ronald J. Glodoski.

A Perigee Book
Published by The Berkley Publishing Group
A division of Penguin Putnam Inc.
375 Hudson Street
New York, New York 10014

Copyright © 1999 by Scott Edelstein
Book design by Lisa Stokes
Cover design by Miguel Santana
Cover photo by Steve Cole, PhotoDisc, Inc.

First edition: July 1999

Published simultaneously in Canada.

The Penguin Putnam Inc. World Wide Web site address is
http://www.penguinputnam.com

Library of Congress Cataloging-in-Publication Data

Edelstein, Scott.
    100 things every writer needs to know. — 1st ed.
      p. cm.
    ISBN 0-399-52508-4
    1. Authorship—Handbooks, manuals, etc.   I. Title.
PN147.E24 1999   99-20096
808'.0—dc21   CIP

Printed in the United States of America

10 9 8 7 6

contents

BUILDING YOUR WRITING SKILLS

MAKING MONEY FROM YOUR WRITING

THE WRITER'S LIFE

What This Book Can Do for You

Welcome. You've come to the place where many of today's new, aspiring, and prospective writers begin—and where many of them learn to become the successful writers of tomorrow.

It's a place designed especially for people who are just starting out in their journeys as writers. And it's also designed for people who haven't yet begun this journey, but who hope to soon—people who need some basic information, inspiration, and guidance in order to take that first step.

It's for people who may be feeling excited, confused, scared, or even all three about the prospect of putting words on paper.

It's a place where you'll find straightforward, down-to-earth answers to your most troubling questions about writing and publishing. Where you'll learn to separate the myths about writing from the realities. Where you'll learn how to discover what most inspires you. Where you'll learn the current realities of the writing business. And where you'll find comfort, inspiration, and encouragement.

This book is a result of my twenty-five years as a professional writer, editor, literary agent, writing and publishing consultant, and writing teacher. During those years I published fourteen books and well over one hundred short pieces around the world. As a writing teacher during those same years, I worked with thousands of people of all ages, backgrounds, and degrees of experience.

Again and again I found that the book so many of my beginning students and clients most needed was a brief, simple, straightforward guide that would speak directly to their most urgent questions and concerns. Unfortunately, for all of those twenty-five years, such a book simply wasn't available.

Finally, I decided to write it myself. You're holding it in your hands now.

Today, at long last, all the guidance that writers most need is available to everyone who writes—or wants to. It's all right here.

100 Things Every Writer Needs to Know is a "first call for help" for every new, prospective, or experienced writer. May you learn from it, enjoy it, find inspiration in it, and use it to become the writer you most want to be.

—SCOTT EDELSTEIN

BASIC WISDOM

■ ■ ■ ■ ■ ■ ■

1
Anyone Who Writes Is a Writer.

Imagine someone were to tell you "You're not a bicyclist until you've ridden at least five hundred miles," or "You can't consider yourself a *real* bather until you've spent at least a thousand hours in the tub." They'd sound pretty foolish, wouldn't they?

Yet some writers and writing teachers persist in trying to tell the world who qualifies to be a writer and who doesn't. "You only become a real writer after you've published three books." "After you've written your first million words, *then* you can call yourself a writer." "Oh, so you have a day job and write at night? You're really a hobbyist, not a writer."

These sorts of pronouncements and judgments are all nonsense—and arrogant nonsense, at that.

If you get on a bicycle and ride, you're a bicyclist. If you fill up the tub and climb in, you're a bather. And if you put words on paper, you're a writer. It's as simple—and as obvious—as that.

How experienced, how talented, and how successful you may be as a writer are other questions, of course. But no matter where you may be right now, you can always gain more experience, nurture the talent you have, and acquire skills that you don't yet have.

In the meantime, it's nobody else's job—or business—to define whether you're a writer or not. And it's not *your* responsibility to live up to that person's criteria.

The words you've put on paper or disc are all the proof you need that you're a writer. And no one else can ever take that away from you.

2 Every Writer Starts Out As a Beginner.

■   ■   ■   ■   ■   ■

All of us begin our educations without knowing how to read. Each of us learns to walk by first learning to crawl—and, later, by falling down repeatedly. And every one of us who writes is or was a beginner at some point.

Being a beginner is nothing to be ashamed of or to apologize for. It's simply an acknowledgment of where you may be right now.

Throughout history, every writer who created something grand and wonderful had to first write dozens, or even hundreds, of pieces that were anything but grand and wonderful. Many of those pieces were utter failures; many were only partially successful. But in each case, the writers learned and grew from them. And because of their mistakes, failures, and experiments, they became better writers. The same will be true of you and your own work.

Actually, in one sense, no writer is ever really a beginner. Most of us were taught to write in elementary school, so by now we've got years or decades of writing experience behind us.

And in another sense, all of us remain beginners no matter how much writing experience we may accumulate. After all, each time you start a new piece, you're bringing into existence something that hasn't existed before.

So whenever you're tempted to look sheepishly at the ground and say to another writer, "I'm just a beginner," catch yourself. Instead, look them in the eye, smile, and say, "I'm a beginner— just like you once were."

3
Some Writers Are Born, But Most of Us Are Trained.

By now the debate is centuries old:

"Writing can't really be taught. It's an innate talent that some people have and others don't."

"That's not true. Writing is a set of skills that people can learn, practice, and constantly build upon."

"Are you saying that anyone can learn to write like Toni Morrison?"

"Are *you* saying that Toni Morrison didn't have to develop her skills to get where she is today?"

The reason this debate continues is that there's some truth to both sides.

There really are some people who seem to be born with natural writing talent—the ability to see things in fresh and unusual ways, and to communicate them with power and grace. Over the years, I've worked with dozens of such people, from kids in first grade to seniors in retirement. I have no idea where their talent comes from, and usually neither do they.

I've also worked with many hundreds of good writers who got where they are through practice, study, and hard work. Some of them took classes; others worked one-on-one with tutors or coaches; and a few confident, disciplined folks pretty much taught themselves.

Dozens of these people have published books, articles, stories, poems, and a wide variety of other pieces. Many are now successful professional writers.

For every writer with obvious inborn talent, there are probably a dozen others who built their skills (and their writing careers) through practice and hard work, one step at a time. Clearly, our world has room for both types of writers.

4 Writing Isn't Inherently Noble, Painful, or Glamorous.

There are rich writers and poor writers; wise writers and foolish writers; happy writers and miserable writers; writers who play polo and writers who raise hogs; writers who hobnob with celebrities and writers who prefer not to leave their homes. Some writers live noble lives; some live painful ones; some live glamorous ones. Others have lives that aren't especially noble, painful, or glamorous at all.

Still, certain stereotypes about writers and writing manage to persist. Like all stereotypes, they are made up of a little bit of truth and a lot of exaggeration and overgeneralizing. Here are the three big ones:

Writing is a noble act. Putting words on paper doesn't make you a better person—or a worse one, either. Writing a novel, a heartfelt memoir, or a twelve-volume epic poem isn't going to advance your moral standing—or your social standing, either.

Writing is painful. (Or its variants: *a writer must suffer; a writer must be unhappy; a writer must be lonely, or neurotic, or crazy; a writer must dwell in nihilistic gloom.*) Some of our best writers are happy, well-adjusted, high-spirited people; others suffer from depression; most—like me—are sometimes happy, sometimes sad or lonely or angry. (It's worth noting that some of the world's most inspiring and uplifting poetry was written by writers who were seriously depressed at the time. And some of the darkest prose ever written was turned out by warm, cheerful, optimistic folks.)

Writing is glamorous. Perhaps one in three hundred writers actually gets to live in glitz and glamor; the great majority of us

9

live humbly and unpretentiously. Furthermore, if you look closely at the lives of those few glamorous writers, you'll discover something interesting: it's not their writing that makes them glamorous, but the wealth and fame that their writing brings them.

As for the act of writing itself, you'll soon discover for yourself, if you haven't already, that it's not glamorous in any way. It fact, it's pretty much the opposite: solitary, intimate, and unimposing.

5
Writing Is an Act and a Process, Not a Definition of Who You Are.

When people hear that you're a writer, some of them will jump to all sorts of conclusions about you. They may expect you to be witty, or cynical, or unreliable; or they may assume you're a night owl, or a beatnik, or an alcoholic.

Do these people a favor. When one of them begins treating you like a stereotype instead of a human being, tell them a few things about yourself that are decidedly unstereotypical. "I love to bowl." "I'm usually in bed by ten o'clock." "I hate berets." Then remind them that "writer" is a description of what you do, not how you live your life.

6 The Only Way to Discover Whether You Have Writing Talent Is to Write.

■ ■ ■ ■ ■ ■

Most beginning writers worry about whether or not they have any talent. They wonder whether all the effort they put into their writing will be worth it, and fear that they're investing their time and energy in something that might have little or no payoff. Some of them want to make sure as quickly as possible that they're not just wasting their time.

There's only one way to adequately address these concerns: *write*. The more you write, the more the answers to all of these questions will naturally reveal themselves to you.

You'll discover for yourself what your strengths and weaknesses are as a writer. You'll learn through hands-on experience what comes easily to you and what gives you the most trouble. And you'll find out what genres, styles, subjects, and parts of the writing process give you the most pleasure.

Don't try to come to any conclusions too soon. Just keep writing, and observe. The answers will emerge on their own.

7
There Is No Single "Right" Way to Write.

Some writers work from seven to nine A.M. every day; others write only when the mood strikes them. Some use computers; others write with red ballpoints on legal pads; still others use voice recognition programs.

Some writers write only about themselves; some write only about other people; some write primarily about animals, or geopolitics, or auto racing. Some start with an image; others with an idea; still others with an outline.

What works for one writer may not work for another. In fact, what works beautifully in the piece you're working on now may not work at all in the one you write tomorrow.

Writing well isn't about following a particular method or philosophy. It's about discovering and making the best choices, piece after piece, line after line.

8
Nothing Will Teach You More About Writing Than the Act of Writing Itself.

If you want to become a good swimmer, get in the water and swim. If you want to become a first-rate cook, get out the pots and pans and start cooking. And if you want to grow as a writer, sit down and write. The more you write, the better a writer you will become.

Reading the work of good writers will help. So will taking classes, attending writers' conferences, talking with other writers, and reading books such as this one. But none of these will do as much for your writing as plenty of practice.

I used to teach writing with Natalie Goldberg, author of *Writing Down the Bones*, *Wild Mind*, and several other books. One day a student asked the two of us a complex and difficult question. I responded first, with a lengthy and detailed answer. Then we all looked at Natalie. She smiled, shook her head slowly, and said to all of us, "I don't know—*just write*."

I can think of no better advice for aspiring writers.

9
Each Writer Builds Their Skills at Their Own Rate of Speed.

If you tend to build your writing skills slowly and steadily, that's fine. If you make little or no progress for a while, then suddenly make a big leap, that's fine, too. Either way, you're growing as a writer.

There's no need to measure your progress against someone else's, or to set arbitrary benchmarks such as "I'll publish a novel by the time I'm thirty" or "If I can't get an A in my poetry writing class, I won't continue with it." In fact, more often than not, these self-imposed comparisons and demands get in the way.

As a writer, you're not in competition with anyone else (or yourself, either), and you're not racing the clock. So relax. Set goals for yourself if you like, but don't make them into absolutes—and don't punish yourself if you don't achieve them.

The point is not to beat out the competition or reach some artificial standard of excellence. It's simply to write as well as you can, and to be willing to learn and grow as a writer. If you make these your goals and simply keep on writing, you'll see consistently positive results.

10

You Can Safely Ignore Most of the "Have To's" You've Been Taught About Writing.

If you'll think back to elementary school, you may remember someone in your class asking, "What happens when you subtract three from two?" Your teacher probably answered, "You can't do that," and showed you with coins or oranges how you can't subtract more than you've got.

Then, a few years later, a different teacher told you about negative numbers, and explained that you *can* subtract a larger number from a smaller one. In fact, this teacher told you, people do it all the time, such as when a business's expenses exceed its income.

Many of the rules you've learned about writing are like the rule of subtraction you learned in first grade. They may still apply in certain circumstances, but now that you're older and wiser, you will come across plenty of situations where they can (and often should) be ignored.

In fact, most of these supposedly absolute rules about writing are merely general guidelines. They make sense much of the time, but can and should be ignored when the situation warrants. Some common examples:

- *Always use standard English.* (Not if you're quoting someone who's speaking in dialect, as in Richard Wright's *Native Son.*)

- *Always use complete sentences.* (Sometimes incomplete sentences will have more power, or sound and feel exactly right. This one, for example.)

- *Never stray from correct grammar, punctuation, spelling, or usage.* (But do use incorrect English if that's how your narrator talks or writes, as in Daniel Keyes's *Flowers for Algernon.*)

- *Never use exclamation points.* (This is a good general rule for scholarly writing, but it doesn't apply to advertisements, comic strips, dialog, and many other writing contexts.)

- *Always rewrite your work, because it can't possibly be good until it's gone through at least two or three drafts.* (What if the energy's flowing perfectly that day? Why rewrite just for the sake of rewriting?)

Other rules about writing have proven helpful for some people, but only get in the way for others. These include:

- *You must write every day, or at the same time each day, or according to a regular schedule.*

- *You must write a certain number of words, pages, or hours each day.*

- *You must have a separate room—or at least a separate space—where you write.*

- *You must be free of all distractions when you write.*

- *You must bare your soul in your writing—or write about the deepest, darkest, most private things you can.*

- *You may work on no more than one piece of writing at a time.*

- *Always write an outline of your piece before you begin writing your first draft.*

- *You must know how a piece will end before you begin writing it.*

- *Always write your title first.*

- *Never rewrite except when an editor asks you to.*

Then there are those "rules" which were useless or absurd in the first place—but which a teacher, parent, or boss may have insisted that you follow. Some common examples:

- *Never write in the first person, use "I" or "me," or use yourself as your subject.*

- *Never start a sentence with "and," "but," "however," "anyway," "nevertheless," or "therefore."*

- *Never use curse words, slang, colloquialisms, or foreign words in your writing.*

- *Never use italics or boldface.*

- *Put the most exciting or important moment of your piece at the very beginning, in order to grab your reader's attention.*

The best way to deal with all of these "have to's"—and any others you might come across—is to hold them up to the light of reason and examine them carefully. If any rule or guideline helps you write better or more easily, by all means follow it. But if the rule gets in your way, then set it aside without guilt, worry, or lengthy deliberation.

11 Outfit Yourself with a Few Basic Reference Volumes.

As a writer, you will find the following volumes very helpful. Most are available in both bound and CD-ROM form. Because they are reference books, you don't need to read them from cover to cover; simply keep them on your shelf and use them whenever necessary.

- A good, complete dictionary. An unabridged one is ideal. Just about any one will do, though I'd avoid the *Oxford English Dictionary*, since it is a dictionary of British rather than American English.

- A large, thorough thesaurus. (Unlike a dictionary, which provides definitions of words, a thesaurus lists words with identical or similar meanings. For example, under the word "corridor," my thesaurus lists "aisle, couloir, entrance hall, entranceway, foyer, hall, ingress, lobby, passage, passageway.") I strongly recommend *Roget's 21st Century Thesaurus*, edited by Barbara Ann Kipfer (Dell), which is excellent and inexpensive.

- An easy-to-use guide to the rules, conventions, and niggling details of the English language. The two best such volumes are *The Gregg Reference Manual* by William A. Sabin (Glencoe/McGraw-Hill) and *Harbrace College Handbook* by John C. Hodges (Harcourt Brace).

- At least one reference volume of general information. I recommend the annual *World Almanac and Book of Facts*

(World Almanac Publications) and *The Concise Columbia Encyclopedia* (Houghton Mifflin/Columbia University Press). More comprehensive encyclopedias, such as *Compton's* and *Encyclopaedia Britannica*, are available on CD-ROM for $40–$80.

- If you have trouble with spelling, you also may want to own *Random House Bad Speller's Dictionary* by Joe Kay and Jordan (Random House). This little volume lists words alphabetically according to their most common misspellings, and provides their correct spellings.

You don't need to rush out and buy all of these tomorrow. But because you'll probably find yourself referring to all of them fairly often, do acquire them as soon as you reasonably can.

12

To Get the Most Out of Writing, Write What You Would Enjoy Reading.

One of the biggest debates among writers and writing teachers goes like this:

WRITER A: *You have to know your audience well or you can't write for them. If you don't keep your audience carefully in mind, you may turn out something that nobody wants to read.*

WRITER B: *You've got the process backward. Serious writers don't pick an audience and then decide how to reach them. They begin with a vision and the energy to render it into words. Only after that vision has been transformed into a literary work do they ask, "What audience will best respond to what I've written?" Furthermore, at that point the question isn't about how to write the piece, but where to have it published or performed.*

WRITER C: *You've both got me scratching my head. I don't always have a vision when I start writing. Half the time I start with nothing but a blank page and a vague idea. How can I think about my audience as I write, if I'm not going to know what I have to say until I've written a couple of drafts?*

All three of these viewpoints are legitimate, because each one reflects the creative process of many writers.

Some writers—especially writers of nonfiction—find it helpful to imagine themselves inside the head of a hypothetical ideal reader. Then they ask themselves, "What does this person feel? What do they want and need from me? What are they expecting or hoping for? What are their fears, their hopes, their desires, and their worries? What do they already know and not know about my subject? What do they need to know that they don't know already? What interests them? bores them? excites them? infuriates them?"

On the other hand, some writers do their best work when they forget about trying to empathize with anyone else. They let themselves be led by their own vision or instincts. (As researcher and writing professor Susan Miller has pointed out, writing can be generative: sometimes a literary work reveals itself to its author as they write.)

Yet all three types of writers share something fundamental in their approaches: *They all write things that they themselves would want to read.* All of them understand that if *they're* not interested in what they're writing, no one else is likely to be.

I'm not big on rules, but if I had to pick the single most important rule for writers, it would be this: *The more interested you are in what you're writing, the more interested your reader will be.* A writer who is fascinated by their subject, no matter how seemingly unpromising, has a good chance of writing engagingly about it. This is partly why John McPhee can write fascinating essays about geology, and Nicholson Baker can write a funny and delightful novel (*Room Temperature*) about commas.

Joseph Campbell said, "Follow your bliss." I'd add, "And your obsessions, too."

One last thought on the subject: If you're ever at a loss as to what to write about, ask yourself to imagine the one story, essay, poem, or book that you'd most like to read. Then write it.

13 Getting Published Isn't Hard, But Getting Published in Prominent Places Is.

■　　■　　■　　■　　■　　■　　■

Once you tell people you're a writer, the question you're most likely to be asked is, "Have you published anything?" If you're like most new writers, you'd like to be able to say, "Of course."

Getting that first piece in print really isn't that hard—if you follow these guidelines:

1. *Write nonfiction.*

2. *Start out with small publications* such as weekly small-town and suburban newspapers, weekly or monthly neighborhood newspapers, other local publications, organizational newsletters, and special-interest publications (e.g., magazines published for stamp collectors, weavers, dog trainers, etc.). In general, the smaller a publication's circulation, the easier it is be published in it.

3. *Make sure that what you've written is appropriate for the publication's readers.* Your neighborhood newspaper is not going to be interested in an essay on brain surgery, no matter how well written it may be (unless, of course, something about the essay has a neighborhood connection).

4. *Don't expect much (or any) money.* Most small publications pay their writers a pittance, half a pittance, or nothing but a handful of free copies.

I don't mean to suggest that you shouldn't write fiction, poetry, or TV, movie, or play scripts if you want to; or that you should avoid sending your work to high-circulation national magazines; or that you shouldn't expect to receive fair market value for your work. I'm simply saying that if rapid publication is your goal, then writing nonfiction for small, low-paying publications is the fastest and easiest way to achieve it.

In contrast, it's usually quite difficult to get published in well-known, large-circulation publications such as the *New York Times*, *Sports Illustrated*, *Vogue*, *Ms.*, *Harper's*, and the *Paris Review*—more difficult, in fact, than most new writers realize. In large part, this is simply because there's so much competition: for every freelance piece each of these publications buys and prints, it rejects hundreds. Furthermore, much of the writing these magazines publish is written by staff writers, or by writers with whom the editors have long-standing relationships. (The same publication/rejection ratio holds true for large book publishers such as Knopf, Norton, Doubleday, Random House, and Simon & Schuster.)

Does this mean you shouldn't try to publish your work in well-known publications? Of course not. By all means shoot for the top (or the middle) if you're so inclined, even if you've published nothing at all. But don't expect much success. For every author I know who hit it lucky early on, I know of dozens and dozens more who succeeded only by starting out small, then building their careers and reputations step by step.

14 Being Published Doesn't Make You a Better Writer or Person.

■ ■ ■ ■ ■ ■ ■

Being published for the first time is a lot like losing your virginity: until it's happened, it may seem like an urgent and almost un-attainable goal. After that first time, however, getting published no longer feels like such an earth-shaking event.

Many beginning writers yearn almost desperately to be pub-lished. Some fantasize about it. While there's nothing wrong with either yearning or fantasizing, it's important to keep the whole experience in perspective.

Getting published doesn't automatically mean you're a great writer, though it probably does mean you're at least a competent one. And being published that first time is unlikely to have a pro-found effect on your life. It almost certainly is not going to make you rich, famous, or more sexually attractive, and it won't make you any wiser or more talented.

On the other hand, it will probably make it a little easier for you to be published again, particularly by the same editor, because your work will be taken a little more seriously.

There is one thing that might change significantly once you've been published: the attitudes of friends and family members. This is particularly true if your publisher is well known and widely respected. Suddenly the same people who made jokes about your writing may treat you with new respect. Your spouse, who might have told people for years, "Oh, her hobby is locking herself in the basement and typing," might suddenly being telling people, "Have you heard? My wife's essay just got published." This new respect won't turn you into a better person, but it will probably feel awfully good.

15

Beware of Anyone Who Wants Money from You to Read, Represent, or Publish Your Work.

■   ■   ■   ■   ■   ■

The writing and editing business has its share of crooks and con artists who prey on new writers' lack of experience and desire for publication. Usually they have a slick sales pitch, nice stationery, and a well-designed brochure. But they surely do *not* have your best interests in mind.

I strongly urge you to avoid all of the following:

- Any literary agent who demands a fee to read your work and consider it for representation.

- Any agent who will represent you only on a fee-for-service basis (i.e., who charges, say, $50 per submission rather than a percentage of what they earn for you).

- Any publisher that wants to publish your work, but requires you to pony up some or all of the costs of publication.

- Any anthology editor who accepts your work, but refuses to give you even one free copy of the book on publication. (But—surprise!—you can buy the book at the special pre-publication price of $50 per copy.)

- Any publisher that puts display ads in newspapers, magazines, or the Yellow Pages proclaiming "Manuscripts Wanted" or "Publisher Seeks Authors."

- Anyone who makes unsolicited contact with you and offers—for a fee—to help you publish your work or improve your writing.

- Any writing contest that involves an entry fee.

Are there exceptions to these rules? Certainly—but they are relatively few and far between. (Some common exceptions include writing tutors, instructors, coaches, and manuscript critics, all of whom will read and respond to your work for a fee. These professionals provide legitimate services for those writers who genuinely need or desire what they have to offer.)

In chapters 79–84 (pages 198–211) I'll discuss the most common scams and schemes in much more detail.

16 Unless You're Rich or Have Substantial Savings, Don't Quit Your Job to Become a Freelance Writer.

A freelance writer (or freelancer) is a self-employed writer who runs their own writing business. If you are willing to work hard, be patient, and persevere in the face of repeated rejection, it's quite possible to become a full-time, self-supporting freelance writer. Certainly many others have succeeded in doing so. You must realize, though, that the process normally takes five to eight years.

The first two years are usually the toughest. During this period, most writers make little or no money, and get turned down 80–100 percent of the time. Typically, things begin to click toward the end of the second year, and thereafter most writers steadily build their careers and increase their income.

The process is a lot like putting the space shuttle into orbit: half the fuel is expended just getting it off the ground and into the air. But once it's in the sky, it doesn't take much energy to keep it speeding upward or settle it into a stable orbit.

Because the first few years of freelancing can be so difficult, don't consider leaving a job cold turkey to become a freelancer. Instead, plan to make the transition gradually over a period of several years. Consider some interim options such as these:

- Reducing your hours at your current job.

- Working the same number of hours, but squeezing them into four long days, so that you have one day a week free for your writing.

- Rearranging your schedule so that you work part of the weekend but have some time available for your writing during the week.

- Arriving and leaving work significantly earlier or later. This frees up some time during the regular business day for your writing business, and also saves on commuting time.

- Quitting your job (at the right time) to take something else part time.

- Quitting your current job and working as a temp or contract worker. This can provide an excellent balance between steady income and flexibility of hours.

There are two circumstances in which it might be a good idea to simply quit your job and begin freelancing: 1) if you've put aside four years' worth of income for your family to live on while you build your new career; or 2) if you already have a *substantial* number of clients waiting in the wings to purchase your work or services.

Of course, if your goal is to write full time, being a freelancer isn't your only option. You may instead want to set your sights on a salaried job as a writer or editor. For more information on this topic, turn to chapters 85 and 86 (pages 212–15).

17

Ask Yourself Honestly What You Want to Get Out of Writing. Then Make That Your Goal.

■   ■   ■   ■   ■   ■

There are dozens of good reasons to write. Some are financial, some emotional, others spiritual. Following is a list of the most common reasons:

—To express yourself.
—To earn money (or get rich).
—To grow as a writer or person.
—To help your readers grow.
—To pass on knowledge or wisdom to others.
—To feel good.
—To move others.
—To communicate your ideas, emotions, experiences, concerns, and obsessions to others.
—To connect with others.
—To connect more deeply with yourself.
—To test out your ideas.
—To explore particular themes or subjects.
—To experiment with different forms, approaches, and genres.
—To see whether writing is enjoyable for you.
—To see if writing might be a suitable career for you.
—To have fun.
—To give satisfaction or pleasure to others.
—To provide catharsis for whatever is inside of you.
—To keep yourself (and/or your readers) sane.
—To persuade others to take your point of view.
—To help establish your reputation, authority, or expertise in a subject.

—To build a career and/or a reputation as a writer.
—To pass the time enjoyably.
—To create something wonderful or artistic.
—To see in print something you've always wanted to see.
—To leave your mark on the world.
—To set other people straight on certain issues or topics.
—To impress others, or to earn their approval, respect, or admiration.
—To escape your everyday reality, and/or to help readers escape theirs.
—To reveal the truth about something.
—To create something significant to pass on to people you care about.
—To prove to yourself, or to others, that you have writing ability.

Any one of these alone is a legitimate reason to write. Most of us write for several of them. Some of us write for them all.

Whatever your reasons are, be honest with yourself about them. If you like, write them down—and post them above your desk if you feel like it. Whenever writing becomes difficult and frustrating—and there will be moments when it will—look back at your list to remind yourself exactly why you write and what you get from your writing.

This knowledge can help you to stay focused. If you find that you've strayed from your own goals, then stop, carefully examine what you're doing, and work to bring your writing back in line with those goals once again.

Incidentally, there *are* some genuinely bad reasons to write, such as:

—To make yourself or others miserable.
—To get revenge.
—To hurt, libel, or defraud others.

—To avoid working, or supporting your family, or some other important obligation.

If you're writing for one or more of these reasons, stop!

18

If You Don't Like What You're Writing—Or the Act of Writing in General—You Can Always Stop.

Unless it's required for your job or a class, writing is always a choice, not an obligation.

If you're working on a piece and you're not happy with how it's turning out, you don't have to finish it. Put it aside for a while and come back to it later—or file it away indefinitely and move on to something else. It's not a sin to abandon a writing project. Very few professional writers finish everything they start; indeed, many of the best writers have whole file drawers of unfinished pieces.

If, after trying your hand at writing for a while, you discover that you don't really enjoy it that much, feel free to stop. You don't need anyone else's permission, and you don't need to feel any guilt or regret. In fact, congratulate yourself, because you've learned something important about your likes and dislikes. You're not a quitter or a "failed writer"—just someone who's following your own inclinations. Let go of writing and, if you like, try your hand at something else.

And if someday you decide you want to start writing again, go right ahead.

THE WRITING PROCESS

. . . .

19 Each Person's Writing Process Is Unique.

■   ■   ■   ■   ■   ■   ■

Some writers carefully outline each of their pieces before they begin writing it; others don't bother with outlining at all. Some begin with the first scene or image, then write the piece in the exact sequence in which they intend it to be read; others write the final scene or stanza first, then work backward. Still others compose the easiest parts first, then fill in the gaps.

Some writers write the same piece from a variety of angles or viewpoints, then pick the one that works best; others select a viewpoint before they write a single word. Some spend days, weeks, or even months pondering before they finally sit down to write; others just sit down (or stand up), begin writing, and see what happens.

Each of these is an example of a writing process. With time and experience, each writer usually develops their own such process.

Developing your ideal writing process can dramatically improve the quality of your writing. It can promote the flow of ideas, words, images, and energy; help you to write your most moving, engaging, or convincing work; and make the act of writing as pleasurable and energizing as possible.

Below are some suggestions to help you discover your own ideal writing process:

- Experiment. Try out different variations and approaches. Note what works and what doesn't.

- Listen to your heart and gut. Your intuition usually knows what will work and what won't (though sometimes it may be maddeningly silent). When something feels intuitively right, go with it.

- When you find the words and images and energy are flowing smoothly, stop *very briefly*, and ask yourself how you got there or what you did to make it happen.

It's important to remember that no single writing process works for everyone. Your ideal writing process is as personal, and as unique, as your fingerprints. That's why you'll need to discover your own, rather than follow someone else's.

One final word on the subject: Some writers don't have a single process at all, but vary it according to the piece they're working on, how far along they are with it, how much or little trouble they're having with it, and what their instincts tell them. If this is what works best for you, do it without hesitation.

20
Discover the Times, Places, and Circumstances That Help You Write at Your Best.

You can do a great deal to energize and support your writing by paying attention to where you write, when you write, and the tools you write with.

It should seem obvious that you would want to write in circumstances that are pleasant, comfortable, and supportive of creativity. Yet many writers don't take the trouble to provide themselves with good—let alone ideal—working conditions. Fortunately, that's a mistake you're not going to make.

Here are some elements to consider:

Time. At what time of day are you most alert? most energetic? most calm? most creative? most free from distraction? (Many writers with families work early in the morning and/or late at night, because those are their best—or only—opportunities for silence and privacy.)

Location. Some writers work best in their attic or basement or guest room. Others like to write in coffee shops, restaurants, parks, or planes. At least one writer works while in the bathtub; another writes while perched on a tree limb. American literature scholar Robert Daly takes his laptop out into the woods and writes while seated on a rock.

Design. Is your workspace inviting and easy to work in? Is it a reasonable size? Is it the right temperature? Does it look and feel comfortable?

Lighting. Do you prefer the room light or dark? Should the light come straight down or over one shoulder? Do you work best with incandescent, fluorescent, halogen, or natural light?

Privacy. Do you need a separate, almost sacred space to write in? Or will activity actually inspire and energize you? (Jane Austen used to write while sitting in a room full of gossiping guests.)

Background sounds. Some writers work best in silence, or with the sounds of birds, surf, or traffic in the background. Others like to hear a hubbub in the next room or outside their window. Some writers play recorded tapes of birdsongs or waterfalls; some drown out all background noise with an electric fan. Many writers like to listen to music, or even TV shows, as they write. (I wrote portions of this book while listening to the rock group The Clash.)

Position. Do you do your best when you're sitting in a hard-back chair, sprawled on the floor, leaning against a wall, or tilted back in your recliner? Is your keyboard at the right height and angle? Is the center of your monitor at eye level?

Furniture. Is your chair comfortable and the right height? Does it provide enough back support? Is your desk big enough to spread out all your notes and drafts?

Writing tools. Each writer has their own long list of preferences here. Do you prefer a computer, a typewriter, a cartridge pen, or the ballpoint you bought last summer with just the right thickness and heft? Do you like plain white copy paper, legal pads, spiral notebooks, or blank bound books? Do you prefer to dictate your first drafts, using voice recognition technology or a dictaphone? (My own preferences are an IBM computer with Microsoft Works; a black-and-white monitor set on 70 percent zoom; and a black, medium-point ballpoint for editing hard copy.)

Food and drink. What kinds of food and drink will give you pleasure, inspiration, and energy while you work—without making you wired, cranky, sleepy, or fat?

Inspiring images or objects. Some writers have posters, poems, prayers, pictures of their partners or families, art objects, flowers, and miniature Zen gardens near their desks. Other writers prefer an open window with an interesting or relaxing view. The late Isaac Asimov preferred a stark, blank, white wall. (I have an illustration of a barefoot young woman seated next to a typewriter, her feet up on her desk. She looks very calm and relaxed. The caption reads: *We don't* care *how they do it in New York.*)

Animals. Writers keep tropical fish, birds, gerbils, rabbits, ferrets, and a variety of other creatures in their offices; others shoo out all the family pets for maximum privacy. I usually write with one of my cats nearby.

Preparation. Some writers get into the right frame of mind by beginning with a brief prewriting ritual lasting five to fifteen minutes. This might involve watering plants, sharpening pencils, cleaning their workspace, changing into their writing clothes, looking over their work from the previous session, or retyping the last page of their current project.

There are no wrong preferences for any of these, of course. Do whatever works, and feel free to experiment as necessary.

If what does work for you happens to be quirky or even downright weird, that's just fine, so long as it doesn't harm anyone. Friedrich von Schiller wrote at his best when his office was filled with the smell of rotting apples. Thomas Wolfe wrote standing up, using the top of a refrigerator as his writing desk. Mark Twain wrote in bed.

Don't be afraid to indulge your own whims in support of your writing.

21
Some Writers Find It Very Helpful to Keep a Journal or Notebook.

■   ■   ■   ■   ■   ■   ■

A journal (or writer's notebook) is a blank book in which a writer records ideas, observations, images, quotations, feelings, impulses, questions, and anything else that seems interesting or pertinent. Some writers use their journals as places to experiment with lines, stanzas, characters, or scenes; others compose drafts of entire pieces in their journals. In all cases, though, the journal serves as a repository for raw material which the writer can mine later on.

As you can see, a writer's journal is a practical and inspirational tool—and it is quite different from a diary, which is simply a personal account of one's thoughts and life.

A journal can take many forms: a bound blank book, a spiral notebook, a three-ring binder, or a computer disc or file. Some writers carry their journals with them wherever they go, so as not to lose an idea when it appears; others keep their journals in a safe place, jot their ideas down on scraps of paper in the flurry of the moment, then transfer those ideas into their journals later on. Some people write in their journals at the same time (or for the same amount of time) each day; others use their journals only when the spirit moves them.

Many writers find journals (and "journaling," the process of writing in them) very helpful. But many other writers don't bother keeping notebooks at all, and do just fine without them.

Personally, I've never kept a journal, and probably never will. I do, however, keep track of ideas and observations in another way—by jotting them down on scraps of paper and filing them in file folders according to subject. Apparently a fair number of other writers do this as well.

You Can Start Work on a Piece of Writing Almost Anywhere—With an Event, a Person, a Quotation, an Image, an Idea, a Setting, or Just About Anything Else.

Damon Knight once said that he begins each of his pieces with the title. The late Philip Dick began his novel *The Man in the High Castle* with an idea: what if Germany had won World War II? William Faulkner's novel *The Sound and the Fury* began with an image Faulkner had of a small child climbing a tree. (That image appears in the middle of the book.) Ursula LeGuin's *The Left Hand of Darkness* also evolved from a single strong image—one of two people walking together, pulling a sled through a snowy wasteland.

You might begin your own next writing project by creating a place, a character, a mood, or a mystery to be solved. In fact, you can start your piece with *anything*—a joke, a sound, a smell, a paradox, or a problem—so long as it leads you (and ultimately your reader) deeper into your material.

Incidentally, despite what some writing teachers may say, you *don't* have to begin your piece with a moment of high tension or excitement. ("My God!" Susan shrieked as she opened the closet door. "It's a dead body!") In fact, such openings often strike readers as heavy-handed and artificial.

23 You Don't Have to Know Where Your Piece Is Going When You Begin Writing It.

■   ■   ■   ■   ■   ■

It's okay to just start writing and see what happens. Indeed, often a piece will reveal itself to you as you write—one scene, stanza, sentence, or line at a time.

For some writers, in fact, it's *not* knowing where a piece is heading that's most exciting and inspiring. This "not knowing" means they're open to a variety of directions, as well as to inspiration and direction from many different internal and external sources.

Nevertheless, some writers do feel they need to work by planning and outlining each piece carefully, then following their own outlines. If you happen to be such a writer, feel free to ignore the advice in this chapter.

24 You Don't Have to Write Your Piece in the Same Order in Which People Will Ultimately Read It.

■   ■   ■   ■   ■   ■   ■

Writing isn't like playing a violin solo before an audience, where everyone hears every wrong note you play. With writing, no one gets to see any of your words until you decide to let them. In the meantime, you have the right—and the opportunity—to change and rearrange those words however you like. Here are some of your options:

- Start with the section that's most vivid or urgent in your mind, or that's most fun to write. Then build around it.

- Write your ending first, then build up to it (or work backward from it).

- Write a variety of scenes or sections; then spread them out, look them over, and see how they fit together. Then write the sections that fill in the gaps.

- Write a section or scene that comes *before* the place where your piece will begin, to help you become familiar with your characters, plot, or setting.

- Start by writing your piece in the order in which the events in it occur—but then skip ahead or backward whenever you need to.

Literary works don't often emerge in the shape and order in which readers will experience them. Usually they'll appear piece by piece, and it will be your job to arrange those pieces into a successful whole.

25 To Help Structure Your Piece or Organize Your Ideas, Try Outlining or Netlining.

Outlining doesn't necessarily mean organizing your ideas into lettered and numbered sections. An outline can be as formal or informal, as loose or structured, as you please. Indeed, an outline can be anything that lays out in condensed form the themes, structure, or overall direction of a literary work.

Some common types of outlines include:

- An annotated list of scenes or sections, with notes on each section. (You might, for example, have a separate page of notes for each section, and on each page you might list key events, images, lines of dialog, points of conflict, etc.)

- A list of central themes, ideas, topics, or plot lines, with notes on each one.

- A highly condensed version of your piece, written as a single continuous narrative. (Here's an excerpt from one such outline: "Ellen comes home to find her husband gone and his wedding ring on the table. She calls her best friend, Tish, who says, 'Thank God he's gone. Congratulations!' The two agree to meet for dinner.")

- A narrative description of what your piece will do or be.

- A flow chart showing the movement of characters, events, topics, themes, images, and/or relationships from the beginning of your piece to the end.

An outline is essentially a road map to follow as you write. It can keep you focused and on track, and it frees you from having to keep every detail about your piece in your head. (Nevertheless, you are always free to alter your outline at any time, or even abandon it entirely.)

Most writers who use outlines prepare them before they first begin writing. But you may also find it helpful to begin writing without an outline—then, when you come to a natural stopping point (or if you get stuck), make an outline *of what you've already written*. This will help you see at a glance what you've done so far, what key themes and images have emerged, and in what direction your piece seems to be heading. It will also help you chart your course as you continue working on the project.

One alternative to an outline is something called a **netline** or **mindmap**. This is far more visual than a more traditional outline, and it is based less on sequence than it is on relationships among the different elements of your piece.

Here's how to begin a netline:

In the center of a sheet of paper, write down the central premise, image, point, event, or character of your piece. (If your piece will have two or more such central elements, put them all near the center, an inch or two apart.) Make each of these a hub. Then, around each hub, write down other images, ideas, points, or events that relate to it.

Finally, draw lines to connect related elements. If an item naturally connects to two or more others, as will often be the case, draw a line to each one.

The resulting netline will be a highly visual diagram of exactly what your piece will embody and involve.

Three sample netlines appear on the following pages. The first is for an essay on prison overcrowding; the second is for a poem about an affair between a chef and her assistant; the third is for a story about an eight-month-long failed romance.

Do you *have* to outline or netline something before you write it? Of course not. Like any other tool, an outline should be used only if and when you find it useful.

Nevertheless, some writing teachers insist that outlining is a necessity for every serious writer. This is usually because it's a necessary part of their own writing process—and they can't imagine that anyone else's process could possibly be different. Like most other one-size-fits-all pronouncements, such advice is best ignored.

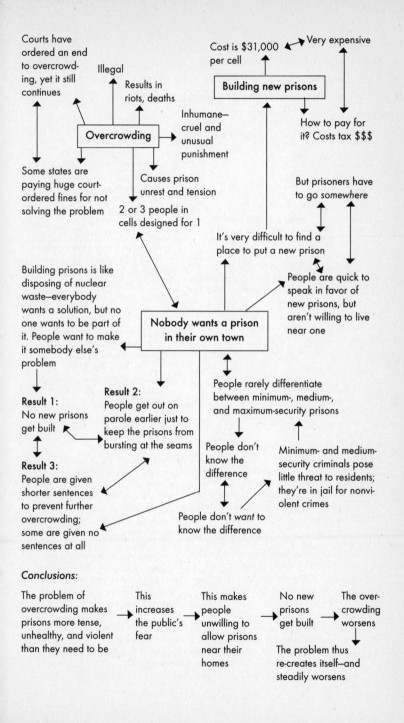

Courts have ordered an end to overcrowding, yet it still continues

Illegal

Results in riots, deaths

Cost is $31,000 per cell

Very expensive

Building new prisons

Overcrowding

Inhumane—cruel and unusual punishment

How to pay for it? Costs tax $$$

Some states are paying huge court-ordered fines for not solving the problem

Causes prison unrest and tension

But prisoners have to go *somewhere*

2 or 3 people in cells designed for 1

It's very difficult to find a place to put a new prison

Building prisons is like disposing of nuclear waste—everybody wants a solution, but no one wants to be part of it. People want to make it somebody else's problem

Nobody wants a prison in their own town

People are quick to speak in favor of new prisons, but aren't willing to live near one

Result 1:
No new prisons get built

Result 2:
People get out on parole earlier just to keep the prisons from bursting at the seams

People rarely differentiate between minimum-, medium-, and maximum-security prisons

Result 3:
People are given shorter sentences to prevent further overcrowding; some are given no sentences at all

People don't know the difference

Minimum- and medium-security criminals pose little threat to residents; they're in jail for nonviolent crimes

People don't *want* to know the difference

Conclusions:

The problem of overcrowding makes prisons more tense, unhealthy, and violent than they need to be

This increases the public's fear

This makes people unwilling to allow prisons near their homes

No new prisons get built

The overcrowding worsens

The problem thus re-creates itself—and steadily worsens

Narrator is Susan, a middle-aged master chef and restaurant owner.

She hires Mario as her kitchen assistant. He is 29, just out of chef's school. His first career was as an accountant.

1. She interviews him for job, tells him *her restaurant's her whole life,* asks why he gave up accounting. He says, "I wanted to sink my hands into something. I wanted to honor my body and tongue." She hires him.

POEM FOCUSES ON THEIR AFFAIR.

2. Mario's smart and talented and quick. Too quick—his second day on the job, in a hurry, he knocks a handful of change into a mixer. He thinks he got all the coins out, but next morning, eating a muffin, Susan bites into a quarter.

3. Five nights later, a huge group of wealthy people arrives just before closing. They spend lots of money, love the food, stay hours past closing time, leave a $50 bill as a special tip for the chefs. Susan asks Mario, "How should we split this?" He suggests a bottle of Dom Perignon from the cellar, at cost. They drink it and get tipsy. He spills champagne on her neck, says, "If you close too early you can lose your best customers," leans forward, kisses her. They fall onto the counter, sending menus flying.

4. Their affair continues in the restaurant. They leave notes for each other on blank restaurant checks about when and where to meet to make love: *party room, 2 P.M.; the meat locker; the roof.* On the roof, they picnic on paper-wrapped chicken, then let their clothing drop away. Afterward, she asks him to take her home with him. He balks. She forces the issue; finally he says, "I can't."

FOOD   MONEY   SLIPS/SHEETS OF PAPER   SPILLING/DROPPING   MOUTH/TONGUE

5. They close up the restaurant for the night. He kisses her and leaves. Feeling ashamed, she follows him home, already knowing what she'll find. From a distance, she sees his wife and kids come outside to greet him, carrying what looks like a birthday cake. She drives away.

6. Next day, doing accounts, she realizes the restaurant is losing money. Mario appears behind her, places his hand on her shoulder. "I doubt you're even breaking even," he says. "Too many cooks." She removes his hand and asks, "Where's your wedding ring?" He steps back, shrugs. "I took it off to make sausage a year ago. Never saw it again." "Why did you seduce me?" "I wanted you."

7. Three days later he quits; he's taken a job as a sous chef across town. He tries to kiss her goodbye; she refuses, hands him his final paycheck. "You should have a professional look over those accounts," he says, and goes.

8. After interviewing people for Mario's job, she hires a talented middle-aged woman. She calls her second choice, a man in his thirties, tells him apologetically that she's given the job to someone else. He thanks her, hesitates, then asks her out to dinner. He pauses again, asks, "Or are you busy cooking every night?" "Of course not," she says. "*Do you think this restaurant is my whole life?*"

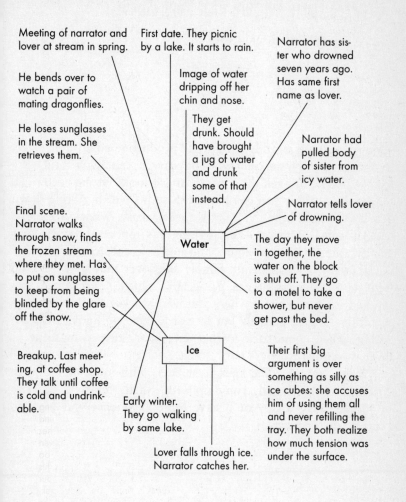

Meeting of narrator and lover at stream in spring.

He bends over to watch a pair of mating dragonflies.

He loses sunglasses in the stream. She retrieves them.

Final scene. Narrator walks through snow, finds the frozen stream where they met. Has to put on sunglasses to keep from being blinded by the glare off the snow.

Breakup. Last meeting, at coffee shop. They talk until coffee is cold and undrinkable.

First date. They picnic by a lake. It starts to rain.

Image of water dripping off her chin and nose.

They get drunk. Should have brought a jug of water and drunk some of that instead.

Narrator has sister who drowned seven years ago. Has same first name as lover.

Narrator had pulled body of sister from icy water.

Narrator tells lover of drowning.

Water

The day they move in together, the water on the block is shut off. They go to a motel to take a shower, but never get past the bed.

Ice

Early winter. They go walking by same lake.

Lover falls through ice. Narrator catches her.

Their first big argument is over something as silly as ice cubes: she accuses him of using them all and never refilling the tray. They both realize how much tension was under the surface.

26 When You're Not Sure What Word, Phrase, or Image to Use, Skip Over It.

You're writing steadily and well, producing page after page. Then, suddenly, the right word or phrase escapes you. You write it once, twice, or even three times, and it looks wrong each time. Or maybe nothing you come up with seems worth writing down at all. Or, worst of all, you draw a total blank. What do you do?

Answer: Don't stop—keep writing! It's important to keep your energy and momentum going, and not to get distracted by what is essentially a small detail. Simply skip over that spot. Pick up with the next line, sentence, paragraph, stanza, or scene.

Leave a blank space where you were stuck, or write or type a blank line, or temporarily put in words that you know are inadequate. Then come back to that spot later, after your scene or draft is finished.

When you do come back to it later, with more of the piece written, you may easily come up with exactly the right thing to do. At the very least, you'll have more experience and focus to bring to the problem.

27
Write More Words Than You Need— Then Cut the Excess Later.

As you write, many different ideas, images, phrases, and options will occur to you. Sometimes you'll come up with two or more different—but equally valid—ways to say or do the same thing. Or you'll envision two or more alternative approaches, each one with a somewhat different emphasis and tone. Or you'll want to explain or describe something in more detail, but aren't sure whether it's really necessary.

Question: Which option do you choose, and how do you make the right choice?

Answer: *Choose all of them.* Write down all the different variations, one right after the other, and continue writing. Don't stop to try to get it exactly right. Keep the flow of words coming.

Later on, when you have the time and energy for it, you can go back, peruse the different options, choose the best one, and get rid of the others. (Or you might combine two different options into something better still, or compose something entirely different, or save an option for another piece.)

28
Be Willing to Take Risks and Make Mistakes.

■   ■   ■   ■   ■   ■

Good writing isn't a matter of mere technical correctness. It needs to be moving, engaging, and convincing, and it needs to provide your reader with an experience, not merely knowledge and correct form.

In fact, most writers do their best work if they don't worry about technical correctness as they write. They know that getting caught up in the small details can distract them or break their momentum. Instead of trying to fix every little mistake as they write, they focus on what's most important: getting their words out onto the page or screen.

It's not that the details of sentence structure, grammar, and punctuation aren't important. It's just that they are best dealt with as you edit and polish your final draft—not while you're in the throes of creation.

But what about larger mistakes? Shouldn't you avoid using the wrong viewpoint, or emphasizing the wrong details, or taking a scene in the wrong direction?

Surprisingly, the answer is no. You *shouldn't* try to avoid mistakes as you write, because you won't know that they're mistakes until you've made them. (In fact, they're not really mistakes at all in the sense of violating some technical rule. They're just attempts at achieving a certain effect—attempts that ultimately don't succeed.)

Writing is usually a matter of feeling your way, line by line and page by page. Much of the time, you simply won't know whether something will work until after you've written it.

Many writers say that this willingness to experiment, to test out ideas, to write alternate versions, and to go in unusual and uncharted directions often leads to their best writing.

Remember, since no one else will see what you're writing until you decide to show it to them, you're in an ideal position to experiment. You have nothing to lose, and there is no one to punish you if what you try doesn't work—and you have a great deal to gain if it does.

29
Ignore the Perfectionist, the Worrier, and the Nitpicker Inside Your Head.

■   ■   ■   ■   ■   ■

All of us have them: the internal voices that tell us we're screwing up, worry that our writing is worthless, and wonder why we're bothering in the first place.

Then there's the voice that's never satisfied—the one that questions every choice we make, and wants us to keep working on the same piece forever, until we get everything exactly right.

The good news is that these voices are normal. They don't mean you're crazy, or neurotic, or not cut out to be a writer. They're standard background noise, like the traffic outside your window.

But they can be distracting and demoralizing nevertheless. And it seems as if the more you try to argue with them or hush them up, the louder and more strident they become. That's normal, too.

So what can you do about those voices? *Keep writing in spite of them*. Treat them like the background noise they are, and simply ignore them. Don't try to prove them wrong or push them away. Let them chatter away, and go on about your business of putting words on paper or disc. You'll discover that when you don't give those voices your attention and energy, after a while they'll slowly fade away, until they're just a low whisper.

Unfortunately, they'll probably never go away completely. (Even after thirty years of professional writing, I still hear those same voices myself, muttering and complaining softly in the back of my head.) Eventually, though, they'll become nothing more than mental Muzak.

30
Virtually All Writers Need to Revise and Edit Their Work— Often Many Times.

Although it happens occasionally, it's quite rare for a literary work to emerge full-blown from a writer's mind. It's much more common to create an initial draft, and then rewrite parts or all of it—in some cases multiple times. Even then you may still need to edit the piece carefully, line by line and word by word, until you can declare it finished.

Rewriting (also called **revising** or **revision**) is the process of looking at all or part of your piece again, and creating a new version of it. This might mean writing a new draft entirely from scratch, or it might mean using what you've done so far as working notes for creating the next version.

When you revise, you're dealing with the largest concerns: tone, pacing, characters, plot, central images, believability, overall structure, and so on. Most writers continue to revise until they get these key elements working the way they want them to.

Editing is the process of looking closely at each individual paragraph, stanza, sentence, line, word, image, and punctuation mark, and then adjusting the language as necessary.

Editing normally begins only after all major revisions are complete and your major concerns have been addressed. (After all, why bother with the small things when some of the large ones still need to be dealt with?)

Polishing is another word for minor editing. (If you do several rounds of editing, the final round is typically considered polishing.)

Proofreading is a final read-through of an otherwise finished piece in which you check spelling, sentence structure, grammar, and accuracy.

Writing, then, is really a series of interrelated processes: thinking and planning, outlining or netlining, composing, revising, editing, and proofreading.

A **draft** is nothing more than a version of a piece of writing. A **first draft** is your first version, a second draft is your next substantially new version, and so on. Your **final draft** is your finished piece. When you simply change a few words here and there, you're not really creating a new draft, but editing an existing one.

How many drafts are enough? Sometimes a single draft, carefully edited, will do the trick. Other times you may have to write many different drafts until you feel your piece is complete. Two to four drafts is typical. (By the way, don't automatically assume that the more drafts you do, the better your piece will be. That thought can keep you working on the same project for the rest of your life. Once you've taken care of all the big things, it's probably time to stop rewriting and move on to editing.)

Sometimes certain parts of the same piece will need more work than others. For example, maybe the first few stanzas of your poem will need nothing more than some judicious editing; the third and sixth, however, will need to go through two or three versions; and the fourth and fifth will sound and feel wrong until you've rewritten them at least half a dozen times.

Some of our best writers write consistently awful first drafts. But they're skilled and patient enough to go back and work with what they've done, sometimes many times, improving it each time.

For this reason, never be ashamed or embarrassed by a work in progress—and don't try to compare it against someone else's finished work. Would you compare your bowl of uncooked pancake batter against someone else's hot-off-the-griddle pancakes?

31

Read Your Work Aloud After Each Draft—and As You Edit.

■ ■ ■ ■ ■ ■ ■ ■

Using your ears as well as your eyes enables you to revise and edit from two perspectives instead of one. You'll be astounded at how many things your ear will catch that your eye has missed, and vice versa.

In general, I recommend reading aloud fairly slowly, so that the sound and meaning of each word have time to sink in.

If editing and reading aloud at the same time are difficult for you, try reading your work into a tape recorder. Then play back the tape, stopping it when necessary, and edit as you listen. (Another option: Have someone else read your piece aloud to you.)

32

Put Your Piece Aside Overnight Before Each Round of Revising or Editing.

Most writers do their best revising and editing when they are able to take a step back from their work, read it objectively, and respond to it as if it were written by someone else. Unfortunately, this can be hard to do when a piece is still fresh in your mind.

To avoid this problem, put your piece aside for a while—at least overnight, preferably for a day or two, ideally for a week or more—before you begin any new round of editing or revising. This gives the most recent version time to fade from your memory. If you do this, when you pick up the piece later and reread it, you're able to respond only to the words on the page, rather than to the images and thoughts that were in your head when you wrote it.

33
The Final Decisions on Writing, Revising, Editing, and Publishing Anything You've Created Are Yours and Yours Alone.

This is both your privilege and your responsibility. Other people can give you advice, suggestions, feedback, and criticism, but no one else can decide how much (or how many times) to revise and edit your work. No one else can determine when your piece is finished. And no one else can decide for you whether to offer that piece for publication.

Do feel free to ask people you trust for their opinions and reactions, of course. But never do what they say merely because they said it, or because they're famous, or because other people agree with them. Famous writers, respected writing teachers, and large audiences have all been known to make some very unsound judgments.

How do you know when a piece is done? There's no single, obvious answer to this question, but usually a piece is finished when it reads right when read silently, sounds right when read aloud, and feels right when read either way. Another clue that your piece is complete: Each time you edit it, you find yourself making only a small number of changes.

When you've reached either of these points, consider the piece done. If you like, send it out for publication; or read it aloud to friends or family; or make it part of a public reading of your work; or put it up on the Net (where it will probably be read, copied, and sent to others); or simply give yourself a thumbs-up and file it away.

34
It's Fine to Work on More Than One Piece at a Time.

Some writers do their best work when they focus on a single piece at once. Most writers, though, are very much the opposite: They have several (or more than several) pieces going at once, and they switch from one to another as the spirit moves them. Usually these pieces are in a variety of different stages.

Either of these approaches is valid, of course. But if you find yourself jumping from piece to piece without ever finishing any of them, then you may have a problem. You can address it by setting a goal of finishing at least two pieces over the next two or three months. Work hard to reach this goal, and don't let yourself be deterred from it. If you get stuck, try some of the strategies for getting unstuck in chapter 36 (page 65).

35

Some Writers Develop Their Own Distinct Style; Others Change Their Style from Piece to Piece.

Lots of good writers have built careers (and substantial follow-ings) by creating their own unique voice and approach. Molly Ivins's work, for example, reads like no one else's—and the better she gets, the more identifiable her voice and approach become. The same can be said of Emily Dickinson, Ernest Hemingway, P. J. O'Rourke, Dave Barry, and hundreds of other writers. Each one has used a unique, easily identifiable voice and approach to carve out a place for themselves among readers.

But there's a down side to this. Once you've established a reputation with a certain style, voice, or approach, it's hard to switch. Readers and publishers will strenuously encourage you to keep doing more of the same.

Then there are those writers who pride themselves on their flexibility, and their ability to change their voice, style, and approach from piece to piece. Typically, these writers write in a number of different genres or for a variety of different audiences. Examples here include Edgar Allan Poe, Langston Hughes, and Joyce Carol Oates.

The positive side of this approach is that these writers develop wide-ranging interests and skills. Because they are so flexible and acquire such diverse writing experience, they can succeed at a great variety of projects and have a relatively easy time becoming full-time professional writers. On the other hand, they may have a more difficult time developing a following than writers whose styles are clearly and immediately recognizable.

Which option should you choose? Whichever one most suits or appeals to you. And there's nothing wrong with using your own special style or approach most of the time, but departing from it whenever the piece you're working on requires it.

36

"Writer's Block" Has Many Different Causes—And at Least As Many Solutions.

■   ■   ■   ■   ■   ■   ■

"**W**riter's block" is a temporary inability to write—or to write well. Most writers experience it at least a few times in their lives, and a small percentage encounter it frequently.

You've got writer's block if:

- You sit down, stare at the empty page, and simply can't get started.

- You're able to get started, but invariably grind to a halt and can't get started again.

- You find yourself stuck at a particular place in your piece, unable to move through it or work around it.

- You write as easily and fluidly as ever, but what you write simply isn't any good. (This is rare.)

- You can't bring yourself to sit down to write at all.

Writer's block can last anywhere from a few minutes to several decades. Usually, though, it only lasts a few hours or days. It is almost never serious; in fact, for some writers it's a natural and necessary part of their writing process. (More on this later.)

Except in its most extreme cases, writer's block isn't anything to fear or worry about. It can usually be cured with a little attention and effort. And even when it can't, it usually goes away by itself after a few days—a week or two at the outside.

Much of the time, you'll find that writer's block is caused by stress in your personal life, such as difficulties at work, conflict with a family member or loved one, financial troubles, grief, depression, serious disappointment, or worry. In these situations, the best way to handle writer's block is to deal with the underlying situation. That might mean resolving it, letting go of your fears or worries about it, or giving yourself time to work through your feelings.

There are physical causes of writer's block as well, such as overwork, illness or injury, drinking or drug use, poor diet, seasonal affective disorder, lack of sleep, or lack of exercise. In fact, any significant change in your eating, sleeping, or exercise pattern can sometimes bring on short-term writer's block. Again, once you've addressed the underlying cause, the block usually dissolves automatically.

Medications and other treatments can also affect people's ability to write. Sometimes just changing your dosage, frequency, or treatment (with your doctor's approval, of course) can get your writing flowing again. (This worked for me when I stopped taking antihistamines for my hay fever and began taking stinging nettle instead.)

Sometimes the conditions under which you work can affect your ability to write. Is the place where you write uncomfortable, badly lit, or poorly ventilated? Is it too cold, warm, noisy, or quiet? Adjust your conditions so that they're as comfortable and conducive to writing as possible, and your writer's block may vanish.

If none of the above solutions works or seems appropriate, then chances are your writer's block truly is writing related. In that case, there are dozens of other effective strategies for helping you get unstuck. Try any or all of the following:

- Just before you begin to write, turn off the ringer on your phone and turn the volume on your answering machine to zero.

- Establish some ground rules for your family regarding your writing time. Make it clear that you are not to be interrupted for anything except an emergency. (You will have this boundary tested almost immediately, and perhaps repeatedly, so hold firmly to it from the start.)

- Exercise, stretch, do yoga, meditate, or pray for a few minutes before you begin writing.

- Create a ritual that you complete just before you sit down to write. This can be as easy as sharpening pencils or straightening your desk, or as serious as reviewing everything you've written on your piece so far. (Important: Your prewriting ritual should last no more than fifteen minutes. Otherwise it may actually get in the way of your writing.)

- Change where, how, or when you write. Write in bed, or in the kitchen, or early in the morning before everyone else gets up.

- Use different writing equipment. Instead of a computer, use a legal pad and a pen, or a manual typewriter, or an artist's sketch pad and a blue magic marker.

- Break your writing time into brief sessions of thirty to sixty minutes each.

- Establish a regular time—or a regular schedule—for your writing. Follow it as religiously as possible.

- If you think you're pushing yourself too hard, ease off. Add breaks, or follow a lighter writing schedule.

- If you're not pushing yourself hard enough, increase your writing time or frequency.

- If you haven't been keeping a journal or notebook, start one. If you have been keeping one regularly, stop for a while.

- Promise yourself something you really enjoy—a long walk, a hot bath, a wonderful meal, a movie—once you've finished your piece (or draft, or difficult page). Keep your promise to yourself.

- End each day's writing in the middle of a sentence or line.

This gives you an obvious starting point for next time—and a chance to build some writing momentum quickly.

- Rewrite or retype the last page, paragraph, or stanza you've written, then keep going.

- Write a letter, a notebook or journal entry, or something else that comes easily for a while. If you like, concentrate on a completely different piece. When you're ready, return to your original project.

- Print out your piece in an unusual and very large typeface, such as 15-point Impact. If you like, print it on colored or designer paper. Then read it aloud, slowly. When you come to the point where you're stuck, begin writing.

- Skip over the spot where you're having trouble, and write a different portion of the piece—even the very end, if you like. Continue skipping around, writing the parts that come most easily and naturally. Then fill in the gaps as necessary, saving the most difficult parts for last.

- Outline or netline what you've written so far, as described in chapter 25 (pages 46–51), then see what direction or ideas the outline suggests.

- Start your section or piece again. This time, write it from a different point of view, or with a different focus, or in a different setting. Experiment with alternative approaches until you find one that works.

- For a set period of time (I recommend twenty minutes), write steadily and continuously, even if you're going nowhere. Write whatever comes to mind, no matter how seemingly irrelevant or silly, and keep writing no matter what. If nothing at all comes to mind, write "nothing comes to mind" over and over until something does. When you're done, carefully look over what you've written.

- Review your old notebooks, journals, and/or other pieces in progress for inspiration.

- For half a minute or so, concentrate on the piece or spot you're stuck in. Then, for the next fifteen to thirty minutes, let your mind wander. Follow it as it wanders, and see what it comes up with.

- Do the exercise in chapter 39 (page 94–96). Look over the lists you create, and see if any item inspires you or suggests a solution.

- Try the creative meditation exercise in chapter 40 (page 97–99).

- Make a list of all the possible directions your piece can go. Include any idea that comes to mind, no matter how silly or unlikely. When you've got a list of at least a dozen—or when you've been working on the list for half an hour—stop and read it over, aloud. Try out whatever ideas feel promising.

- Ask a writer friend to read what you've done so far and suggest some options or ideas. Or ask them to continue your piece for you, writing a few paragraphs or lines where you left off. Then take it from there yourself.

- Take your attention off your piece for a while. Instead, watch a movie, take a walk, or clean your garage. If necessary, stop writing altogether for a few hours—even a day or two. (Sometimes you'll actually need to take your conscious mind off the problem in order to allow your unconscious to find a solution.)

- Set the piece aside, but promise yourself that you will return to it at a specific day and time in the future. Mark that day and time on your calendar. Keep your promise to yourself when that time arrives.

One last thought on the subject: What looks like writer's block may sometimes be nothing more than your own natural writing rhythm. Many writers simply *can't* write steadily, day after day; they need to go through periods of not writing in order to do their best work. During these periods, they may nevertheless be very much at work, consciously or unconsciously processing ideas and connections.

Look at your own writing rhythms to see if your down times seem to be part of a cycle. If they are, perhaps they are a natural part of your writing process. If that's the case, don't think of those times as writer's block, but as necessary periods of rest and rumination.

37 Never Throw Away Anything You Write.

I don't mean you should save every shopping list or "welcome home" note you write to your spouse. But it is a good idea to save all the creative writing you do—and not just all your finished work (both successful and unsuccessful), but every unfinished scene; every fragment that goes nowhere; every outline or netline that never evolves into a finished piece; and every good image, line, or metaphor that gets cut out as you revise and edit your work.

Why save all these odds and ends? Because you may be able to use them someday. The scene that you removed from one story may provide the basis for another. The overheard conversation that simply wouldn't work in your essay about Hollywood may turn out to provide the perfect opening, eight years later, for an article you write on California culture. The poem about your sister that simply wouldn't come together may suddenly finish itself late one night next summer, after you and your sister have spent the day together. Every one of your scraps, false starts, and dead ends may someday provide you with just the words, ideas, or inspiration you need.

Incidentally, if you use a computer or word processor, I urge you to save all of these bits and pieces as hard copy as well as on disc. It's a lot harder to lose something that's in a file folder *and* a computer file than something that's saved in only one place and format.

BUILDING YOUR
WRITING SKILLS

■ ■ ■ ■ ■ ■ ■

38
Become Familiar with Some Basic Writing Terms.

■　　■　　■　　■　　■　　■　　■　　　■

It's not necessary to study or memorize a long list of terms in order to write well. On the other hand, it's a good idea to be introduced to some of the most common literary terms, so that you'll be able to communicate more effectively with other people about what you write. It's also useful to have a list of these terms available as a reference.

I've provided such a guide to literary terms below. For ease of use, I've broken it into several sections.

FORMS OF WRITING

Creative prose (or **creative nonfiction**) · Usually, a work of nonfiction that uses some of the techniques of fiction, and/or that concerns itself primarily with providing an emotional (rather than merely intellectual) experience.

Creative writing · Writing of any type that is designed primarily to evoke emotions or explore emotional truths.

Fiction · A work of prose that provides readers with an emotional experience, but does not purport to provide a factual account.

Nonfiction · A work of prose that recounts or discusses real events.

Poetry (or **verse**) · Any literary work written in lines and stanzas.

Prose · Any literary work written in sentences and paragraphs.

Script · Any literary work written in dialog and scenes. A script may be written for radio, audio, television, film, theater, or audiovisual presentation.

TYPES OF LITERARY WORKS

Essay (or **article**) · A short work of nonfiction prose focusing on a single topic or set of topics.

Novel · A book-length work of fiction, normally 40,000 words or longer, with a variety of characters, a central plot, and several subplots. A novel usually builds to a climax and resolution near the end. A **docunovel** is a recounting of real (or mostly real) events in a novelistic fashion, using many of the techniques of fiction. Examples: Norman Mailer's *The Executioner's Song*, Bob Woodward and Carl Bernstein's *All the President's Men*.

Novelette · A rarely used term for a short story of more than 10,000 words.

Novella (or **short novel**) · A midlength work of fiction, usually between 20,000 and 40,000 words.

Play · A dramatic work to be performed by live actors. A **radio play** is for voices and sound effects only.

Prose poem · 1) A poem which employs sentences and paragraphs rather than lines and stanzas; 2) a very short prose work, usually no more than 1,000 words, which uses a variety of poetic techniques, such as vivid imagery, assonance, alliteration, consonance, onomatopoeia, internal rhyme, and compression of language.

Screenplay (or **film script**) · Any dramatic work written for film production. A **docudrama** is a type of screenplay (or teleplay) in which real events are presented using many of the techniques and conventions of a fictional screenplay.

Short-short story · A very brief story, usually 1,500 words or less, often with a surprising or ironic ending.

Short story · A brief work of fiction, usually less than 10,000 words. Typically, a short story has a single plot, conflict, and sequence of events, and no more than a handful of characters.

Song · Any work in verse written to accompany music.

Teleplay · A dramatic work written specifically for television.

Vignette (or **study**, or **slice of life**) · A brief literary work which describes or focuses on a single character, occurrence, place, or moment in time. The piece provides an emotional or aesthetic experience for the reader, but normally there is no climax or resolution. A vignette may be a work of fiction or nonfiction.

GENERAL WRITING TERMS

Acronym · A word (or group of characters) composed of the first letters of other words. Examples: *scuba* (self-contained underwater breathing apparatus), *FBI* (Federal Bureau of Investigation).

Active voice (or **active language**) · Writing in which people, organizations, groups, and animals do things and act upon their environments. Examples: *I welcome your comments. Pass me the salt. All four women shook their heads.* The opposite of active voice is **passive voice** or **passive language**, in which events and actions are highlighted, while people are ignored or moved into the background. Examples: *Your comments will be welcomed. The salt was passed. Heads were shaking throughout the room.* With rare exceptions, active language is stronger, clearer, and more interesting than passive language.

Allegory · A story containing characters—and sometimes events, images, and settings—which are meant to be taken symbolically rather than literally. Many of Jesus' sermons were allegories. George Orwell's *Animal Farm* is a modern allegory.

Alliteration · The repetition of the same initial sound in two or more words in the same line, sentence, stanza, or paragraph. Examples: *strewn* and *strong*; *Nicholas* and *narcotic*.

Ambiguity · A passage, scene, or entire piece that can be read in more than one way. When used properly, intentional ambiguity can be a very powerful literary device; an unintentional ambiguity, however, can seriously weaken a passage or piece. A passage containing an ambiguity is **ambiguous**.

Antonym · Word having the opposite meaning of another word. *Huge* is the antonym of *tiny*. Compare with its opposite, **synonym**.

Assonance · The repetition of the same vowel sound, usually in two or more words in the same line, sentence, or stanza. Examples: *best dressed*; *late-breaking news of the nation*.

Automatic writing (or **free writing**) · Writing down whatever ideas, images, and words occur to you, in a single, nonstop, unedited stream. Automatic writing can be a very useful way to create early drafts or notes for pieces. Sometimes incorrectly called **stream of consciousness** (see page 86).

Bibliography · A reference tool, included at the end of an essay or book, which lists all the most important sources consulted by the author.

Book proposal (or **portion and outline**) · A document used by authors to sell their books to publishers before those books have been completed. A typical book proposal consists of one or more chapters, an outline or synopsis of the entire book, a one-page biography of the author, and other relevant items. For a nonfiction book, these might include a table of contents, an introduction, an analysis of the market, an overview of the need for the book, an analysis of competing volumes, and/or endorsements from well-known people. For a novel, a proposal typically consists of one or more sample chapters, plus a narrative synopsis of the entire plot.

Cadences · The pattern of sounds in a literary work, particularly 1) the stressed and unstressed syllables, and 2) changes in volume and pitch.

cf. · An abbreviation which simply means "compare to" or "compare with."

Character · Any person who appears in a literary work. Animals (as in Jack London's *White Fang*), alien beings (as in the movie *Star*

Wars), mythical creatures (as in innumerable folk tales), and robots (as in the movie *Lost in Space*) can all be characters as well. So can ghosts, vampires, werewolves, and even disembodied voices. **Characterization** is the creation, use, and development of characters.

Cliché · Any overused or trite phrase (*cute as a button*), image (*a hippie flashing a peace sign*), or idea (*dogs are loyal*).

Climax · The point of highest tension or conflict in a literary work. A climax is usually followed by a resolution or a shift in relationships. It is possible for a piece to have more than one climax.

Consonance · The repetition of the same consonant sound, usually in two or more words in the same line, sentence, or stanza. Examples: *pear pie*; *cashing in on shame*; *an anthem to the growing throng*.

Context · Situation.

Denouement · The final working out or resolution of events in a literary work.

Dialect · A particular variant of a language. Dialects can be regional (southern; New York), national (British; Jamaican), professional (business; academic), or racial (black American; native Hawaiian). Intonations, pronunciations, grammar, diction, usage, volume, and vocabulary can all differ from one dialect to another.

Dialog (also spelled **dialogue**) · Any verbal discussion between two or more people or characters.

Diction · Proper word choice and usage, beyond the observance of mere grammatical rules. *Please pass the salt* has correct grammar and good diction. *I would feel gratitude if the salt were passed to me by you* is grammatically correct, but has terrible diction.

Draft · A version of a literary work. A **final draft** is a completed piece.

e.g. · "For example."

Ellipsis (or **ellipsis points**) · Punctuation consisting of (usually) three dots in a row. An ellipsis can be used in several ways: 1) to indicate a trailing off or gradual pause (*Well, I'm not sure . . .*); 2) to indicate, by implication, a continuing sequence or pattern (*Forty-one bottles of beer on the wall . . .*); or 3) to indicate that words have been omitted from a quotation (*"I pledge allegiance to the flag . . . with liberty and justice for all."*). When the omitted words include the end of a sentence, a fourth dot is added.

Epiphany · Any moment of insight, realization, or awakening in a literary work. Either a character or a reader can experience an epiphany. (This term has a very different meaning in religious contexts.)

Figure of speech · Any common but quirky (and nonliteral) use of a word or phrase. Example: *That's not my cup of tea.* Virtually synonymous with **idiom**.

First person · Any writing with *me, I, we,* or *us* as the subject. Examples: *Let me see it. I was furious. We know what we're doing. Let us go free!*

Flashback · A scene (or part of a scene) in which the reader is transported out of the literary present to witness an event or incident that took place in the past.

Focus · A vague (but often-used) term that can mean a variety of things, from clarity to emphasis to theme to viewpoint. If it's not clear from the context what someone means by this word, ask them for clarification.

Foreshadowing · A literary device in which events which appear later in the text are implied (or hinted at) through the use of image, dialog, event, or word choice. Foreshadowing can be overt, subliminal, or somewhere in between; often it occurs naturally, without the writer's conscious intent.

Free writing · See **automatic writing**.

Genre · Any major literary form, such as poetry, fiction, drama, nonfiction, etc. The word is also sometimes used to refer to more specialized forms of writing, such as the short story or the documentary film. It can also be used—somewhat confusingly—to refer to still more specialized types of writing, such as fantasy, mystery, or horror (despite the fact that a work of fantasy might be a play, a short story, a novel, a poem, or a film).

Gerund · Any verb that has been made into a noun by adding an *-ing* ending. Examples: *golfing, moving, swimming*. A letter may be dropped or added in the process.

Grammar · The formal rules of language governing speech and writing.

Homonym · Any word that is pronounced exactly the same as another, often (though not necessarily) with a different spelling. Examples: *bee* and *be*; *train* (noun) and *train* (verb); *dear* and *deer*; *bare, bear* (noun), and *bear* (verb).

Hyperbole · Any deliberate (and often extreme) exaggeration used for emphasis or other literary effect. Example: *The desserts here are to die for*. Hyperbole often (but not necessarily) uses **metaphor, simile,** or some other **trope**. Often it is intentionally humorous, and it is almost never to be taken literally.

Idiom (or **idiomatic phrase**) · A frequently used expression that doesn't make literal sense, but whose meaning is widely understood. Examples: *Cut it out! They've got me by the short hairs. The hotel had gone to seed years ago.* (See also **figure of speech**.)

i.e. · "That is." Example: *Final decisions will be made by the accounting department—i.e., Marilyn.*

Image · Any sensory impression, or set of impressions, used in a literary work. An image can evoke any of the senses, or any combination of senses. The use of images is known as **imagery**.

Infinitive · The word *to* followed by a verb. Examples: *to fly; to go; to celebrate*.

Irony · Any result, end, or outcome which is precisely the opposite of what might be expected. Example: a woman from Minnesota goes to Georgia in February to get some sun and warmth, only to arrive in Atlanta during its first blizzard in decades. Irony also refers to any figure of speech whose actual meaning is the opposite of its literal meaning. Example: *Dom DeLuise to Kate Moss: "Hi, Tubby! How's* *the fashion biz?"* The word is sometimes misused to mean surprising, unexpected, pathetic, awful, or extreme.

Libretto · The lyrics to an opera, musical, or other lengthy choral composition.

Lyrical · Musical sounding. Do not confuse with **lyrics** (see below) or with **lyric**, which is a type of poem (see page 92).

Lyrics (or **song lyrics**) · Words to a song.

Metaphor · An image that compares (or relates) one person, thing, event, or idea to another, either directly or by implication. Examples: *Hakim was a bear of a man. The prosecutor chipped away at Terry's story, layer by layer.*

Mixed metaphor · Two metaphors used confusingly or inappropriately together. Examples: *Walk softly and carry a big carrot on a stick. Home is where you hang your heart.*

Monolog (or **monologue**) · An uninterrupted speech made by a person in a literary work. An **interior monolog** or **internal monolog** is the uninterrupted flow of a single person's thoughts on the page. See also **soliloquy**.

Mood · The ambiance or atmosphere of a particular scene, stanza, passage, or literary work. Similar but not identical to **tone**. (In the play *Arsenic and Old Lace*, the tone is cheery but the mood is grim.)

Narrative (or **narration**) · Any sequential recounting of events, normally by a single person or character. A narrative may be written or spoken.

Narrator · The character, person, or voice in a literary work that communicates to the reader. A narrator may be the author themselves (as in Anne Lamott's *Operating Instructions*), a character in the piece (as in Herman Melville's *Moby Dick*), or an unnamed, unseen presence (sometimes called a **disembodied narrator**), as in Edith Wharton's *Summer*, or most news stories in magazines and newspapers. An **omniscient narrator** is a disembodied narrator with superhuman powers—e.g., the power to reveal multiple people's thoughts, or discuss future events (*In a few days, Felipe would be* *proven wrong*), or reveal to the reader information unknown to one or more characters. A literary work may have more than one narrator; in William Faulkner's *The Sound and the Fury*, for example, each section is told in a different character's voice. It is also possible to have no narrator at all, as in James Thurber's "File and Forget," which purports to be an exchange of letters between Thurber and employees of the Charteriss Publishing Company.

Non sequitur · A meaningless, pointless, or irrelevant phrase. Non sequiturs often sound meaningful but boil down to nothing. Examples: *Second place always comes behind first. Make your vote more than a vote.* A non sequitur can also be a conclusion or inference that doesn't really follow from its premises. Example: *Aspirin is 15 percent more effective on pain other than headache—so when you have a headache, take aspirin.*

Onomatopoeia · Words and phrases that sound like what they mean. Examples: *splash, boom, plop, fizz.*

Oral · Spoken aloud (as opposed to written or conceptual).

Oxymoron · A phrase or pair of words that contradicts itself—either deliberately, for literary effect (*Brenda was deeply committed to her ambivalence*), or unintentionally (*jumbo shrimp*). Pointing out unintentional oxymorons—e.g., *military intelligence*—is a frequent source of humor.

Pacing (or **pace**, or **rate of revelation**) · The rate at which events occur in a literary work. If an event takes several pages to play itself out, the pacing is very slow; if a great deal happens in only a few lines, the pace is quite swift. The following has a very rapid rate of revelation: *The next morning, Kim packed her bags and flew to Cairo. A day later she was in Aswan.*

¶ · This symbol simply means "paragraph." When inserted between two sentences, it means "begin a new paragraph here." "No ¶" means "make the previous and subsequent paragraphs into one."

Paraphrase · To restate in different words (sometimes in briefer form). Also, any passage that offers such a restatement.

Parody · A form of humor in which an institution, person, group, organization, event, or philosophy is lampooned through imitation and exaggeration. Example: the magazine (actually, a book that looks like a magazine) *Catmopolitan,* which purports to be a version of *Cosmopolitan* for cats.

Parts of speech · The eight different kinds of words: verbs (*eat, sleep, snore*); nouns (*bottle, religion, Toni Morrison, Nike Corporation*); pronouns (*we, us, her*); adjectives (*redundant, strenuous, green*); adverbs (*boldly, sleepily, pathetically*); prepositions (*above, between, under*); conjunctions (*therefore, but, however*); and interjections (*whoops, oy, eek*).

Pen name · See **pseudonym.**

Phonics (or **sonics**) · 1) The way a literary work (particularly a poem) sounds; 2) The use of sound devices—such as rhyme, meter, alliteration, assonance, repetition, etc.—in a poem or other literary work.

Plot · The sequence of events that occur in a literary work. A longer work may have a primary plot as well as one or more secondary plots, or **subplots.** A plot is not always necessary for a shorter work; many poems, as well as some works of fiction and drama, succeed without clearly defined plots.

Plot synopsis · See **synopsis.**

Portion and outline · See **book proposal.**

Point of view · See **viewpoint.**

Protagonist · The primary character in a literary work. A protagonist may or may not be the **narrator,** and may or may not be the **viewpoint** character. Some works, such as John Steinbeck's *The Grapes of Wrath*, have multiple protagonists; many successful literary works, such as Shirley Jackson's "The Lottery," have no protagonist at all.

Pseudonym (or **pen name**) · A fictitious name used by an author for their byline.

Rate of revelation · See **pacing.**

Re · Regarding. **In re** simply means "in regard to."

Redundant · Repeated unnecessarily. Examples: *100 short, brief recipes*; *He pointed at her, extending his finger in her direction.*

Rhetoric · 1) The use of written or spoken language to persuade or convince others; 2) Empty or overblown words; promises, accusations, or conclusions that lack substance or support. Example: *So far, all the other side has been able to produce is rhetoric.*

Rhythm · 1) In a literary work, the ebb and flow of sounds—particularly stressed and unstressed syllables; 2) Variations in pacing and/or in other aspects of a literary work.

Satire · Humor which makes fun of a person, group, institution, idea, event, organization, or philosophy, typically through exaggerating its qualities.

Scene · A section of a literary work which recounts a single event or series of events. Normally a scene is written from a single point of view.

Second person · Any writing with *you* as the overt or implied subject. Recipes and instruction manuals are usually written in the second person, as is Dylan Thomas's poem "Do Not Go Gentle into That Good Night."

Setting · 1) Location (of a scene, image, stanza, etc.); 2) A description of a place (or a group of images) that establishes a scene's location and ambiance.

Sic · A Latin word, used when quoting another speaker or writer, to indicate that their assertion, diction, spelling, grammar, capitalization, syntax, or punctuation is improper. The word should be placed immediately after the error, in italics (or, if the error itself is in italics, in non-italics) and brackets. Example: *As Mark explained the situation, "My doctor says I have an enlarged prostrate* [sic]."

Simile · Any comparison of one person, event, image, group, or thing with another, using the word *as* or *like*. Examples: *Janine swims like a fish; My poor mother is as deaf as a post.* See also **trope**; compare with **metaphor**.

Soliloquy · A monolog spoken by a character in a dramatic work, usually to the audience (though sometimes to themselves).

Song lyrics · See **lyrics**.

Sonics · See **phonics**.

Stet · An editing and proofreading term that undoes a correction. If you've written in a change by hand, then later decide to undo it, writing "stet" above or beside it tells the reader to ignore the change.

Stereotype · An oversimplified (and, usually, one-dimensional and clichéd) portrayal of a person, group, place, or organization.

Stream of consciousness · A literary technique which presents a person or character's thoughts as they occur. This may be done in standard, straightforward English (e.g., *Oh, God, Marya thought, not this again. This is the last thing I want now*.) or in nonstandard language meant to replicate thoughts (e.g., *Oh God, not again, not again, this is the last thing I want now, can't he see what I'm going through . . . but he doesn't see, the fool*). Frequently, but incorrectly, confused with **automatic writing**.

Subplot · A minor or secondary **plot** which works alongside (or in connection with) a main plot in a literary work. Some literary works have multiple subplots.

Symbol · A literary device in which an object, image, person, or event evokes a meaning other than (or in addition to) itself. The bald eagle, for example, is often used to symbolize the United States. **Symbolism** is the use of symbols.

Synecdoche · A form of **trope** in which an individual stands for an entire group, or a part stands for the whole. Examples: *If you wanted a Betty Crocker for a wife, why in hell did you marry me? Can we get one of those brains from Harvard to help us out?*

Synonym · Word having the same meaning. *Couch* and *sofa* are synonyms, as are *frightened* and *afraid*. Compare with its opposite, **antonym**.

Synopsis (or **plot synopsis**) · A highly condensed summary of a literary work, usually in narrative form. In book publishing, the word **outline** is sometimes used in the same way (see **book proposal**).

Syntax · Sentence structure.

Theme · Any significant point, topic, idea, or concern in a literary work.

Third person · Writing that has as its subject *she, he, it, they*, or *them*. Examples: *He took a step back and groaned. The world needs P. J. O'Rourke; it also needs Molly Ivins. The dog ran after its master.*

Tone · The way a scene, passage, section, or entire literary work sounds (rather than feels). Compare with **mood**. In the work of Edward Gorey, the tone is usually quite grim, yet the mood is grotesquely funny.

Trope · Any expression, phrase, or word used in a nonliteral (and usually representative) manner. Examples of tropes include **metaphor, symbol, irony, simile**, and **synecdoche**.

Usage · The commonly accepted standards, rules, and guidelines for language. These include syntax, diction, grammar, punctuation, capitalization, and spelling.

Verbatim · Word for word.

Verbiage · 1) Excess words; wordiness; 2) Wording, as in *Let's find some verbiage that works for both sides.*

Verbose · Overly wordy.

Viewpoint (or **point of view**) · In a literary work, the perspective through which events are viewed and/or narrated. This perspective can be the author's; a character's; someone who claims to be the author but in fact is a fictional character or voice (e.g., the narrator named Kurt Vonnegut in *Breakfast of Champions*); or a disembodied narrator's (see **narrator**). Many literary works, such as Virginia Woolf's *To the Lighthouse*, are written from multiple viewpoints.

It is possible to write from the point of view of a character while remaining in the third person, as in the following sentence: *Denitra shivered; she knew what was waiting for her at home.*

Voice · The manner, tone, diction, and syntax in which a literary work is written—or in which a character speaks.

POETIC TERMS

Accent (or **stress**) · The natural emphasis placed on a particular syllable. In the word *napkin*, for example, the accent is on the first syllable; in the word *potato*, the second syllable is stressed.

Caesura · A pause or break in the middle of a line. Example: *She wept, and gave thanks.*

Canto · A section of a poem.

Envoy · A concluding stanza which provides a moral, a summing up, or a fresh perspective.

Foot (or **poetic foot**) · Any group of two or three consecutive syllables in a line of poetry. A foot can consist of an entire word (*human*), two words (*a bird*), three words (*I want a*), or part of a word (*unmitigated* contains two feet, an **amphibrach** and a **trochee**). Any line of poetry that's more than a single syllable long contains one or more poetic feet. There are seven different feet, each one reflecting a different pattern of stressed and/or unstressed syllables. These are:

NAME	SYLLABLES	EXAMPLES
iamb	one unstressed + one stressed	surround, I think, the dog
trochee	one stressed + one unstressed	nonsense, ready, throw it
dactyl	stressed + unstressed + unstressed	dangerous, give me a

anapest	unstressed + unstressed + stressed	overwhelm, on a bridge
amphibrach	unstressed + stressed + unstressed	annoyance, my mother
spondee	stressed + stressed	Sioux Falls, go fish
pyrrhic	unstressed + unstressed	of the, with a, so it

See also **meter** below.

Free verse · Poetry written without regular meter or rhyme. Successful free verse does, however, employ other poetic techniques. Most poetry written and published today is free verse. Do not confuse with **blank verse** (see **meter** below) or **automatic writing** (see page 78).

Line break · The spot where a line of poetry ends; the visual pause at the end of a line.

Meter (or **metrics**) · The pattern of stressed and unstressed syllables in each line of poetry. A poem's meter is based on the poetic feet in each line. (Not all poems have meter, or need to. Some poems have both meter and rhyme; some have neither; some have meter but no rhyme. A poem made up of unrhyming lines of iambic pentameter is said to be written in **blank verse**.) A line consisting of a single poetic foot is written in **monometer**.

Most poems consist of lines which utilize a variety of feet. However, if a line uses one particular foot over and over, then it can be identified as follows:

NAME	DESCRIPTION	EXAMPLE(S)
Dimeter	one foot repeated twice	Going steady; a raucous kazoo band
Trimeter	one foot repeated three times	Sally wanted breakfast

Tetrameter	one foot repeated four times	I wish my brother understood
Pentameter	one foot repeated five times	"Nothing doing," Thomas told me, smiling.
Hexameter	one foot repeated six times	"It's me," I said, and handed her the yellowed page.
Heptameter	one foot repeated seven times	Flying to London, I suddenly knew that my journey would take me to Birmingham.

The meter (if any) of a poem or line reflects the number and type of feet in it. A line consisting of four trochees in a row is written in **trochaic tetrameter**; one made up of three anapests in a row is written in **anapestic trimeter**. Sonnets, which contain fourteen lines of five iambs each, are written in **iambic pentameter**. (Most lines of verse include two or more different poetic feet, and thus are said to be written in **mixed meter**.)

Poetic foot · See **foot**.

Prosody · The study of patterns of sound, such as rhyme and meter, in literature (particularly poetry).

Refrain · A repeating phrase, line, set of lines, or stanza in a song or poem.

Rhyme · The repetition of the same sound—either a vowel sound (as in *he* and *sea*) or a combined vowel and consonant sound (as in *vine* and *sign*). A poem's pattern of rhyme is called its **rhyme scheme**, and is usually represented by the first few letters of the alphabet. For instance, imagine a ten-line poem in which lines one, three, five, and seven rhyme; lines two, four, six, and eight rhyme; and the final two lines rhyme. The rhyme scheme for this poem would be *a b a b a b a b c c*. (If those final two lines also rhyme with line one, the rhyme scheme would be *a b a b a b a b a a*.) Some variations on rhyme include:

- **Slant rhyme** (or **half rhyme**): *me* and *beat*; *mate* and *street*; *time* and *mine*.

- **Eye rhyme**: *tough* and *though*; *cafe* and *strafe*.

- **Internal rhyme** (rhyme within a line or sentence, rather than at the end): *She told me she'd hold to her promise.*

- **Masculine rhyme** (the rhyming of final syllables): *correct* and *connect*; *surround* and *profound*.

- **Feminine rhyme** (identical final syllables, preceded by a rhyme): *kitten* and *mitten*; *castle* and *hassle*.

Scan · The act of identifying the number and type of feet in each line of a poem. **Scansion** refers to how a particular poem scans.

Sprung rhythm · A variant of traditional poetic feet, invented (and widely used) by the poet Gerard Manley Hopkins. In sprung rhythm, each foot is made up of a single initial stressed syllable, followed by one or more unstressed ones. When read aloud (or "spoken" mentally by a silent reader), each foot takes up the same amount of time, creating a somewhat musical effect. Here is a sample of sprung trochaic tetrameter: *Jim the bartender offered me soda water.*

Stanza · A group of related lines—the poetic equivalent of a paragraph. A stanza can be as brief as one line or as long as the entire poem. Stanzas are separated from one another by one or more blank lines; this blank space is called a **stanza break**. Stanzas of different lengths have their own names: a **couplet** is a two-line stanza; a **tercet** or **triplet** is a stanza of three lines; a **quatrain** is four lines; a **cinquain** or **quintet** has five lines; a **sextet** or **sestet** is six lines; a **septet** consists of seven lines; and an **octave** has eight lines. (Longer lengths do not have names.)

Stress · See **accent**.

If you're interested in a more detailed discussion of poetic terminology and forms, consult Paul Fussell's excellent book *Poetic Meter and Poetic Form* (Random House; McGraw-Hill).

TYPES OF POETRY

Most poems do not follow a preestablished structure. However, many poems, both old and new, do follow one of the these common forms:

Ballad · A song or poem that tells a story, typically using four-line stanzas that rhyme *a b a b* or *a b c b*. Do not confuse with **ballade**.

Ballade · A highly structured poem consisting of three eight-line stanzas, each rhyming *a b a b b c b c*, followed by a single four-line stanza (or **envoy**), which rhymes *b c b c*. Compare with **ballad**.

Haiku · A brief poem consisting of a single three-line stanza. The first and third lines are five syllables each; the second line is seven. The haiku is a traditional Chinese and Japanese form, but writers in the West have used it as well. Typically, a haiku does not rhyme, and makes use of one or more striking images from nature. Compare with **tanka**.

Lyric · A brief poem, narrated by a single narrator, which expresses one emotion. Do not confuse with **lyrics** (words to a song) or **lyrical** (musical-sounding).

Rondeau · A highly structured poem running on two rhymes, usually consisting of thirteen lines of eight or ten syllables each, and an unrhymed refrain taken from the beginning of the first line. The rhymes and refrain are typically arranged *a a b b a*.

Rondel · A carefully structured fourteen-line poem in which certain lines repeat themselves, word for word. Lines one, seven, and thirteen are identical, as are lines two, eight, and fourteen. A rondel rhymes *a b b a a b a b a b b a a b*.

Sestina · A very rigid and complex form of poetry which contains six six-line stanzas and a final three-line stanza (or **envoy**). In each stanza after the first, the final words of lines one, two, three, four, five, and six are the same as the final words of lines six, one, five, two, four, and three of the previous stanza. The final stanza, which contains only three lines, uses all six of these repeated words. Sestinas normally do not rhyme.

Sonnet · A poem of fourteen lines, organized in one to four stanzas, which follows a rhyme scheme such as *a b a b b c b c c d c d e e, a b b a a b b a c d c d c d, a b b a a b b a c d e c d e*, or *a b a b c d c d e d e d g g*. Each line is written in iambic pentameter—that is, it is exactly ten syllables long, with every even-numbered syllable accented. Many sonnets follow the **Italian**, or **Petrarchian**, form, in which a conflict or problem is set up in lines one through eight; a major shift then occurs, and the final lines present a resolution, response, or answer to the conflict.

Tanka · A classic form of Japanese poetry. A tanka is made up of five lines of five, seven, five, seven, and seven syllables. It usually focuses on a single event, setting, mood, or image (or set of images).

Villanelle · Another rigid and complex poetic form. A villanelle has six stanzas; the first five have three lines each, which rhyme *a b a*, and the sixth has four lines, which (usually) rhyme *a b a a*. Lines one, six, twelve, and eighteen are exactly the same, word for word. So are lines three, nine, fifteen, and nineteen. A traditional villanelle is built around two key words, which appear a number of times in the poem, though often in different contexts or with different meanings. Some conflict or tension usually builds throughout the poem, and is resolved in the final line, which includes both of the key words.

It is of course possible (and quite acceptable) to write poems that are variants of these forms. You might, for instance, write a "sonnet" composed of lines of twelve (rather than ten) syllables, or you might write a haiku-like poem that's five lines long.

39
Get in Touch with What Inspires You.

■   ■   ■   ■   ■   ■

If there is anything resembling a secret to writing well, it's getting in touch with what most inspires you. Here's one simple way to do this:

Sit down in front of a pad of paper, or in front of your computer screen. Take off your watch and put it beside you, in clear view. Close the door if you can, turn off the ringer on the phone, and shoo out any pets and children. Get comfortable. Take a couple of deep breaths.

Now write down the following, in all capitals:

THINGS THAT MEAN THE WORLD TO ME

Look at that phrase for a few moments. When I give you the cue, please spend the next two to three minutes (no more) listing the things, people, animals, ideas, experiences, and sensations that fit this description.

There's no need to describe any of these items in detail. Just write down a word or two for each—enough to identify it.

If you have trouble getting started, or want some suggestions for beginning your list, write down the following three items, all of which mean a great deal to almost everyone:

Sex
Food
Sleep

You don't need to be able to explain (even to yourself) why something or someone belongs on this list. You don't have to be reasonable, logical, or moral, either—just honest.

If you get stuck, or run out of ideas, that's fine—just sit quietly until the next item comes to you.

By way of examples, here are some responses other people have come up with:

My new baby, Aidan
Lake Superior
Falling leaves
Late afternoon sunlight in October
The way my husband whispers naughty words in my ear at three A.M.
The taste of a ripe Haralson apple on a clear, cold November morning
How my cat purrs when she's nestled in the crook of my arm
The sound of church bells on Sunday morning
Geese flying overhead in spring
The sweater my girlfriend just gave me

Ready to write your own list? (Remember, don't take more than three minutes.)

Do it!

When you're done, sit back and look over what you've written.

You've just compiled a short list of some of the things that inspire you. Save it. If you're ever at a loss as to what to write about next, simply grab this list and pick one of the items on it.

You can add to this list whenever you want, using the same process you've just followed (though you can take more than two or three minutes if you like).

Want to discover the things that inspire you in other ways? Use the technique described above, but at the top of the page write one of the following:

THINGS I CRAVE
THINGS THAT DRIVE ME CRAZY
THINGS I CAN'T STAND
THINGS THAT FASCINATE ME
THINGS I'M OBSESSED WITH
THINGS THAT MAKE ME FURIOUS
THINGS I LOVE
THINGS I _____(your choice)

Better yet, start eight new pages, and create a list for each topic.

From now on, whenever you feel like it—or whenever you need to give your writing a jump start—sit down and add to one or more of these lists. Or start a new one.

And when you're not sure what to write next, look through your lists and ask yourself what most inspires you *right now*. Then start writing.

40 Take Time to Meditate and Ponder.

The process described in the previous chapter works primarily with your conscious mind. But you can also get in touch with what moves and inspires you by tapping into your unconscious. Here's one easy way to do this:

As before, find a place where you can sit comfortably and quietly, with few or no distractions. Have paper and pen or a keyboard in front of you.

If possible, keep your back straight and your spine arched forward just a bit. (You can do this by sitting in the middle of the chair, rather than against the back. If this is hard for you, try putting a pillow between your lower back and the back of your chair.) Take off your watch and put it in front of you, so you can easily read the time. Place your hands comfortably in your lap.

Take a few slow, deep breaths. Then let your breath fall into its own natural rhythm.

Focus your attention on your lungs as the air moves in and out of them. Don't try to think of anything in particular—but don't try not to think, either. Just follow your breath in and out.

After a few breaths, move your awareness slowly downward—first to your stomach, then to your center of gravity just below your navel. Feel your belly move in and out slightly with each breath.

Look at your watch and make a mental note of the time. If you prefer, write it down.

In a minute you'll be closing your eyes. Once you do, continue to simply follow your breath as it flows in and out. Don't try to think or not think. When you do find yourself thinking about something, or when a mental image appears, calmly return your attention to your breath once more.

You'll be doing this for ten minutes. When you think ten minutes are up, open your eyes; if fewer than ten minutes have passed, close your eyes again until the time is up.

When you're ready, take one more breath, then close your eyes. When the ten minutes are up, read the section below.

Slowly, pick up your pen or move your hands to the keyboard.

Right now, write down the images and people and ideas that appeared in your mind over the past ten minutes. It doesn't matter what they are or whether you understand their meaning. Whatever came to you, write it down.

Use only a few words for each item. Don't describe anything in detail unless it was particularly vivid or lasted a long time. If an image appeared that was bizarre or frightening or confusing, write it down anyway. If you saw or felt something you can't name, leave it unnamed—just describe it as best you can.

Here are the sorts of things people typically come up with:

The wing of a black bird in flight, pushing up and down
The wrinkles in a smiling baby's fat cheek
A nozzle to a gas pump, gleaming under artificial light
A hassock rolling down a hill
My mother laughing, then screaming, then frowning
A wheel, spinning rapidly, never stopping
Row after row of books, all different colors
The veterans' cemetery near the airport
Cats licking their legs

When you're done writing, look over your list. These are thoughts and images and people that have meaning for you. You may not be able to explain how or why they are meaningful, or even what that meaning is, but that's not important. What's important is that you now have another list of items that move or intrigue or fascinate you in some way.

If you have a strong emotional reaction to something on your list, that's a good sign—it means that item has particular significance for you. (But if something seems too frightening or painful to deal with, feel free to back away from it. This is writing, not psychotherapy.)

You can of course add to this list whenever you wish. And, if you like, you can repeat this creative meditation regularly—once a week, once a day, or simply whenever the spirit moves you. Each time you do it, you'll get more deeply in touch with what matters to you—and each time your list will get a little longer.

41 Fantasize. Ask "What If?"

Whether you're writing poetry, screenplays, science fiction stories, mysteries, erotic novels, or your family history, don't just look at things as they are. Also consider how they might be.

Take any one element of your piece, then ask yourself, "What if this were different?" What if it were more extreme, or more subdued, or exactly the opposite? What if Gianni were ten years older, or less abusive, or stuck in traffic ten minutes longer? What if Shoshanna had a pet ferret instead of a cockatoo? What if the plane were to land at a different gate? What if the scene were written from Jack's point of view instead of Lucy's? What if Aunt Kanh had missed that last plane out of Saigon? What if the cab driver were to get lost in Roxbury? Ask yourself whatever questions most appeal to you. You may be surprised at some of your own answers.

Here's another, slightly different, process for fueling your creativity. At a turning point in your piece—or, if you prefer, at some other spot—ask yourself one or more of these questions:

- What's the best thing that could happen right now?

- What's the worst thing?

- The scariest thing?

- The most painful?

- The most unexpected?

- The most exciting?

- The funniest?

- The weirdest or most incongruous?

Asking these questions can be particularly useful when you don't know where your piece is heading; when it seems to be losing its edge or energy; or when it's starting to bore you.

42 Show Rather Than Tell.

Look at these two passages:

1. Josie was feeling extremely happy.

2. Laughing, Josie threw open the windows and leaned outside. "Attention, residents of Squirrel Hill!" she shouted. "Everyone within hearing distance is entitled to two free drinks at Finnegan's, courtesy of Josie Jesperson, the luckiest woman in the whole state of Pennsylvania!"

Which of the two passages reveals more about Josie? Which has more energy? Which got you more involved? Which was more enjoyable to read?

In the first passage, the narrator simply tells you a fact about Josie. In the second, the narrator shows you exactly what Josie said and did. While the first passage merely explains, the second provides a full-fledged (though fictional) experience.

In general, effective writing shows rather than tells, reveals rather than explains, evokes an experience rather than sums up what happened. It does this by giving readers the same information they would pick up on their own if they were watching and listening. Good writing thus shows people in action—talking, gesturing, running, fighting, making jokes, making mistakes, making love, or making supper.

Are there exceptions to this general rule? Sure. If you're writing a recipe, a news story, an instruction manual, or directions to your uncle's house, your readers don't want or need a vicarious experience—they just need to be told what happened or what to do. And if you need to get a character in your short story from Addis Ababa to Tunis quickly, then by all means write, "The next morning Candice was in Tunis." (On the other hand, you might want to show what Candice feels like when she arrives—in which case you might write, "The next morning she was standing on the hot tarmac of the Tunis airport, jet-lagged, sweaty, and disheveled.")

43 Involve Your Reader's Senses.

We experience the world entirely through our senses. We use the information they provide us with to construct a constantly changing mental image of the world "out there."

The five senses, then, are your tools for creating (or re-creating) the world inside your reader's head. Whether you want your readers to experience the world we live in today, the world of the past, or a fictional world of your own creation, the key to getting them involved is providing them with sensory information.

Look at these two lists of adjectives:

gleaming	enigmatic
scowling	frightening
smoky	gorgeous
slimy	unbelievable
buzzing	ridiculous
salty	tragic

The words on the left all provide sensory information. Using this type of information, you can create a vicarious experience for your readers. For instance: *The custard was at once salty and slimy. Scowling, I put down my spoon. Above me, the neon sign buzzed and flickered. "What's the matter?" Kyoko asked me. "Don't you like fish?"*

In contrast, the words on the right provide no sensory information at all. Instead, they merely provide intellectual judgments about human experience. As such, they are a step removed from reality, a step away from life as we experience it.

To see the difference between the two types of words, compare the above description with this one: *I tried the fish custard. It tasted really awful, unbelievably bad. I despised this restaurant, even its sign. Then Kyoko asked me whether I liked fish or not.*

Which description is more vivid? Which is more involving? Which would you rather read?

All this having been said, the fact is that you don't create a vicarious experience for your reader merely by loading down your work with lots of sensory details. More isn't always better. In fact, good writing is a matter of selecting the most appropriate and revealing details. Compare these two sentences:

1. *The big, brown, growling dog ran up to me and sank his long, sharp, white teeth into my bare, recently suntanned leg just beneath my knobby, wrinkled knee.*

2. *With a growl, the Great Dane leapt toward me. A moment later her mouth closed around my calf, and I felt her teeth sink deep into the muscle.*

I hope it's clear that the second sentence offers the reader a genuine (though fictional) experience, while the first is little more than a laundry list of adjectives.

Any clear sensory detail, or group of sensory details, is called an **image**. Images stick in our minds and hearts, and they are often what give life and power to a literary work.

44 Write Multiple Variations, Versions, or Scenarios.

If a scene, or image, or piece you're writing isn't working, change direction. Move the action to a different time or location; change the viewpoint; or replace one character with another. Have the piece begin at an earlier (or later) time. Try writing versions of your piece in two or more different genres.

Write three or four different versions in all, changing one or more important elements each time. Then read each one aloud, and ask yourself these questions:

- Does one or more of the versions solve the problem I'm having?

- Does what I've written suggest a new, better direction?

- Which version works best?

- Which version should I use—or should I create a hybrid of two or more versions?

Sometimes writing new variations can be helpful even if your piece is turning out just fine. For example, by writing a scene over again from a different character's point of view, you may learn a great deal more about that character. Or you may discover some implications or overtones to the scene that you hadn't seen before. Or you may simply wind up writing a stronger, more moving scene.

Other good reasons to write different variations of the same section or piece:

- You're not sure where your piece should go next.

- You're wondering whether a certain direction or approach might work.

- You want to "test drive" a variety of possibilities before you pick the best one.

- Your natural writing process is to choose from among several options rather than select a direction and then stick to it.

- Writing several versions provides you with a clearer perspective on your piece.

- It gets your creative juices flowing.

- You enjoy doing it.

45 Combine Unexpected Elements.

In creating any literary work, you bring together a variety of images, ideas, and events. Usually these elements go together naturally, or at least belong to the same general realm.

But they don't have to. In fact, one of the best ways to add energy and vividness to a piece is to combine elements that wouldn't normally go together.

In his book *The Act of Creation*, Arthur Koestler calls this process **bisociation**. For Koestler, bisociation (and **trisociation**, in which three diverse elements are combined) is at the very heart of the creative process.

Bisociation can take the form of an image (*a Tibetan monk, dressed in orange robes, bowling*); an event (*a rash of burglaries in which the burglars leave behind handsome calligraphed certificates which read "This home, with the address of_____, was burgled on_____, 1999. What was yours is now ours."*); an observation or insight (*If the black box containing the flight recorder always survives an airplane crash, why don't they make the whole airplane out of the stuff?*), or simply an unusual combination of words (*Poolesville was just another pale, exhausted mining town*).

Bisociation can also form the basis for an entire literary work, such as my own short story "Magic City," in which I combined an abandoned, poisoned city (à la Love Canal in Buffalo) with a high-tech amusement park. In the story, set sometime in the future, the city of Cleveland has become a getaway for vacationers. No one lives there anymore, but robot bag ladies roam the streets; giant rusted factories run at full tilt, manufacturing nothing; and the polluted Cuyahoga River bursts into tall multicolored flames once every hour.

Bisociation and trisociation can give a piece of writing—regardless of its genre or subject—a big jolt of energy. It can shock, surprise, or delight your readers, take them in a direction they hadn't expected, or even widen or deepen their view of the world.

Furthermore, for you, the writer, the process of bisociating can help you discover angles, directions, and options for your piece that you hadn't seen before.

Of course, bisociation isn't just a matter of placing wildly diverse elements side by side. The trick is to create a context in which they can work together. For example, imagine a woman holding a watering can, watering her husband as if he were a plant. Taken alone, that image is vivid and surprising, but ultimately nonsensical (or, at best, merely surreal). But suppose we know that her husband is about to walk in the annual Earth Day parade, and he's wearing a specially designed suit made out of sod. Suddenly everything fits together—yet the image is no less surprising or funny. In fact, because all the elements do fit together, it may be even funnier.

46
Writing Teachers, Classes, and Workshops Range from Wonderful to Outright Harmful.

In the United States alone, well over ten thousand writing classes, workshops, conferences, seminars, tutorials, and correspondence courses are offered each year. These are available through colleges and universities, community centers, writers' centers, libraries, bookstores, community education programs, open universities, art centers, and dozens of other types of organizations. Where do you start, and which course or workshop is best for you?

You start with the teacher. Any class, workshop, or one-on-one critique is only as good as the person offering it. And writing teachers run the full range from supportive and inspiring to absolute poison. (Over the years I've had a chance to see many of my colleagues in action. Some of them I admire greatly; most are mediocre at best; and a few seem to take pleasure in killing their students' enthusiasm and confidence.)

How can you tell if someone is a good teacher? Do a little research. Here are some tips:

1. Talk to the instructor directly, well before the class or workshop begins. This is neither unusual nor difficult to do. Start by asking the registration person for the instructor's phone number. (At colleges and universities, ask the department secretary.) Then call the instructor, introduce yourself, say you're interested in their upcoming course, and ask a few questions. For example:

- "What will be the focus of the course?"

- "What activities will the course involve? Is there reading? In-class writing? Regular writing assignments? Critiquing of one another's work?"

- "Who would you recommend take this class?"

- "I'm a writer of (short stories, plays, romance novels, essays, etc.) and I have ____ amount of writing experience. Do you think your workshop would be good for me?"

- "What will we get out of the seminar? What will each of your students come away with?"

- "What's your philosophy of teaching? Your philosophy of writing?"

- "What about the class most excites you?"

- "Is there a syllabus? Can you mail or fax me a copy now?"

While the specific answers to your questions are important, at least as important (and perhaps most important of all) is the instructor's attitude. If instructors seem helpful, willing to talk, and genuinely interested in their subject, those are all good signs. If they seem primarily concerned with what you will get out of the experience (rather than your obligations to them), that's better still. And if they're friendly, forthcoming, and excited about the class, that's best of all.

On the other hand, if they're standoffish and want to get rid of you as quickly as possible, be concerned. If their comments focus primarily on your obligations in the course rather than the benefits you'll reap from it, be actively worried. And if they're rude, abrasive, or arrogant, have nothing more to do with them.

If the organization sponsoring the course won't give out instructors' phone numbers (as is often the case), don't just go away. Say something like this: "I'd like to learn more about the class before I sign up. Would it be possible to have the instructor call me?" Much of the time, this will result in a call from the teacher.

Another option: If the instructor has regular office hours, make an appointment to meet with them face-to-face—or, if the teacher permits drop-in office visits, just show up.

2. Talk with others who have studied with the instructor. Ask the registration person or department secretary for the names and

phone numbers of two of the instructor's past students; then call those students and ask them for their honest appraisal.

Many organizations routinely request written evaluations on each instructor from their students, and keep these evaluations on file. Ask the registration person or department secretary if you can view these evaluations for the teacher you're interested in.

3. Sit in on one of the instructor's classes for a few minutes. This usually requires the permission of either the organization, the instructor, or both, so ask in advance. (It's fine to simply show up five or ten minutes before a class begins, and explain to the teacher that you'd like to sit in and why.) Don't be surprised or offended, though, if the answer is no. Some instructors feel—quite legitimately—that visitors can disrupt the intimacy of a class; and some organizations have a policy against class visits. If you do visit a class, simply observe; don't participate unless you're asked to (or unless the instructor gives you specific permission to do so).

Once the course or workshop begins, if you're not happy with it or the instructor, bail out immediately! While it's not common, sometimes a teacher who seems great in person may turn out to be a dud or an ogre in the classroom. Most organizations will give you a full or partial refund if you quit after the first session and explain that you were unhappy with the instructor.

While it's pretty obvious what makes a poor teacher, not everyone agrees on what makes a good one. Each writing instructor has their own teaching style—which can be formal or informal, structured or freewheeling, intimate or distant—and the style that works best for one student won't necessarily be ideal for another. Your own ideal writing instructor will not only be a good teacher, but will have an approach and a sensibility that resonate well with your own.

Incidentally, someone's ability as a teacher appears to be independent of how much they've published, how many awards they've received (including awards given for "excellence in teaching"), how famous they are, or how much teaching experience they have. Some of the worst writing instructors I've ever encountered are famous, widely published, and highly regarded. So are some of the best.

47 Get Feedback on Your Writing from People You Trust.

If you're like many writers, you can benefit a great deal from other people's responses to your work. Their critical feedback can help you:

- Discover the ways in which a particular piece you've written succeeds—and the ways in which it currently does not.

- Solve problems or dilemmas you've been facing with your writing.

- Determine how to proceed with a work in progress.

- Identify your own strengths and weaknesses as a writer.

- "Test market" pieces that you feel are finished, or close to it.

- Learn about good places to publish your work.

It doesn't make much difference whether people critique your writing by phone, in person, in a letter, or via e-mail. What *is* important is that the reactions come from people you trust. These people could be other writers, writing teachers, professional manuscript critics (see below for tips on selecting one), friends, your spouse, or other family members.

A good manuscript critic:

- Is honest and forthright.

- Is willing and able to address both the strengths and the weaknesses in your writing.

- Looks at your work on its own terms, not according to some predetermined idea of what good writing should be.

- Is clear about their own biases or preferences (and we all have them).

- Has your own growth and best interests at heart.

- Naturally resonates with what your work attempts to do.

This last qualification is especially important, because no literary work can ever please everyone. Each piece that you write will have its own natural audience (though that audience won't always be easy to define). *Your critic must either belong to that audience or be able to imagine themselves a part of it as they read your work.* Otherwise, you'll be getting feedback from someone who is out of tune with what you're trying to do. This means, for example, not showing your romance novel to a writer of literary fiction, or your essay on the benefits of big government to a Libertarian, or your punk porn thriller to a retired high school principal.

Incidentally, while it's always nice if your critic has a background in writing or literature, it isn't strictly necessary. Any intelligent and thoughtful reader who fits the criteria above should be able to provide you with helpful feedback.

Some writers seek out feedback from people they already know; others join or form a writers' group; and still others purchase a critique from a professional manuscript critic. If you choose to go the third route, keep in mind the following:

- Professional critics, like writing teachers, range from extremely helpful to actively harmful, with every step in between.

- Fame, awards, important publications, and a job at a prestigious university do not necessarily make someone a good manuscript critic—or a bad one, either. Don't pay much attention to these external credentials.

- Before you hire any paid critic, interview them briefly by phone. Find out how they work; what they charge; how they charge (by the hour, page, or project); what sorts of projects they specialize in; and what sorts of material they have worked with before. Tell them a little about your project, and ask them if they feel they have the right background and expertise to work with you on it. Ask them for the names and phone numbers of other writers whose work they've critiqued—and by all means check those references before you hire them. Lastly, ask yourself whether you feel comfortable with this person.

- Feel free to shop around. Talk to two, three, or even several paid critics before you make your choice. Don't be afraid to compare prices—or to mention one critic's price to another. (On the other hand, don't just shop for the cheapest price.)

- To find a professional manuscript critic, try calling writers' centers; arts resource centers; college and university English and writing departments; and the literature departments of very large libraries. Ads for paid critics also appear in many writers' magazines and newsletters.

- If anyone promises you that their critique of your work will guarantee you publication, or representation by a literary agent, they are lying. Have nothing to do with them under any circumstances.

Is it okay to have more than one person critique your work—even the same piece? Absolutely. You don't need to be "loyal" to any one critic, any more than you need to buy gas at the same gas station every time.

48

Consider Carefully What Others Have to Say About Your Writing—But Never Let Their Comments Overrule Your Own Judgment.

When getting feedback on your writing, your role is not to argue or explain or defend yourself. Instead, simply listen (or read). Take notes if you like; answer any questions the critic may have; and ask whatever questions may be on your own mind. But mostly just pay attention to what they have to say.

Some of their comments will probably make sense to you. Some of them may not. Either way, simply take note of them and keep on reading or listening.

Then, later on, alone, look back at your critic's comments. Consider them carefully and thoughtfully, one by one, each on its own merits. Ignore any claims to authority based on reputation (*"I say this as a distinguished professor of literature with six books to my name"*) or consensus (*"The editor of any important literary magazine would surely agree with me"*). Then accept whatever comments and suggestions make sense, and ignore the others.

Never follow someone else's advice simply because you paid for it, or because they're famous or highly respected, or because they're convinced that they're right. There is only one good reason to take someone else's advice: because it makes sense to you.

Because the piece is yours, you and you alone are the final authority on anything you write. You don't have to justify or explain your decisions to anyone. You don't have to apologize for them. And you shouldn't feel guilty about them.

Are there any exceptions to these suggestions? Actually, yes. You may sometimes need to do what someone else says in order to keep your job or succeed in school. In these situations, however, simply be clear with yourself about why you've temporarily given up your authority. You're changing what you've written not because your boss or instructor is right, but because your circumstances require it.

49 Follow Your Heart and Gut.

Your brain is smart, but your heart and gut are wise. Listen to them.

When you have an intuition about what to do next in a piece you're writing, follow it—even if your brain urges you to do otherwise. Your gut will usually know what's right for the piece. At the very least, its promptings will usually lead you in the right direction.

And when you're unsure about where to go or what to do next with your piece, look to your heart and gut (as well as to your brain) for answers. The meditation exercise from chapter 40 (page 97) will help connect you with the wisdom of your own subconscious.

50 Let Your Writing Find Its Own Way.

Ultimately, only you can discover your own unique direction as a writer.

Books, articles, workshops, classes, conferences, and mentors can all help you become a better writer. They can help you publish your work, make money from your writing, and even build a writing career. But none of them can tell you (or has the right to tell you) what direction your writing, your career, or your life will take. Those choices are yours and yours alone.

Yet life is surprising. Some writers set a course for themselves, follow it, and wind up exactly at their goal. Others start out the same way, but find themselves veering off in unexpected directions. A full-time journalist starts a short story, just for fun; it slowly grows into a novel, sells half a million copies, and launches her on a new career as a fiction writer. A technical writer is unexpectedly offered a gig ghostwriting a famous entrepreneur's autobiography; the entrepreneur is so pleased with it that he offers the technical writer a full-time ghostwriting job. Writers as diverse as Amy Tan, Dave Barry, Robert Fulghum, and Alexs Pate have all built careers in one direction, only to find themselves (very happily) pulled in another. Sometimes your best-laid plans may get washed away—yet the results may be far better than anything you anticipated.

There are times to stick to your program, times to modify it somewhat, and times to abandon it for something new or better. So be observant, and be flexible. If a new direction emerges, don't automatically turn away from it. Instead, consider it carefully. If it feels right, be willing to change your course, at least temporarily.

The same holds true for any individual piece you're writing. You might begin it with a clear structure or ending or plot in mind, only to find it turning into something else entirely. A minor character suddenly begins to take center stage. The mansion in Maine slowly turns into a villa in the Italian countryside. The editorial that begins by attacking the President's policies toward China ends by sympathizing with him and acknowledging his difficult position.

When this happens, it's usually a good sign. It means your piece is speaking to you, guiding you, helping you shape it into what it needs to be. Don't tune out that help and try to force your piece back into its original mode. Instead, welcome the guidance, and listen to it carefully. It's usually right on the money.

The late John Gardner said that a literary work is the master and its writer is the slave. If you're serious about writing, he advised, do whatever your piece demands.

That's good advice.

MAKING MONEY
FROM YOUR
WRITING

▪   ▪   ▪   ▪   ▪   ▪   ▪

51 Understand the Difference Between a Salaried Writer, a Contract Writer, and a Freelancer.

There are four basic ways to make money from your writing: 1) get a job as a writer; 2) hire yourself out as a contract writer— i.e., a temp in the field of written communication; 3) sell your work to publishers and/or producers; and 4) sell your services as a writer to businesses, nonprofits, and/or individuals on a freelance basis.

The plusses of taking a salaried job as a writer are a steady income and—for full-timers—paid benefits. On the minus side, you must write what you're told to write, and your job may closely resemble any other nine-to-five office job.

Contract writing offers a bit more flexibility. As a contract writer, you work for a contracting service, which finds you assignments lasting from one week to two years. The pay is often substantially higher than it would be for a similar salaried job, but usually there are no paid benefits. There is also far less security, since there is no guarantee that the contracting service will place you in an assignment when you want one. On the up side, you have the freedom to take time off between assignments or to turn down assignments that don't appeal to you. Each gig is different, which provides variety, but also uncertainty—and the risk of ending up with an unpleasant assignment. Sometimes you may be able to work out of your home and/or select your own work hours; for other assignments you may need to dress formally, commute to an office, and work nine to five, five days a week.

Freelance writers have far more flexibility, independence, and self-determination than either of the other two groups. They enjoy far more freedom in the hours they work, where they work, and the way they dress. Yet they also must handle a high level of uncertainty. They must arrange and pay for their own health and disability insurance, and they never get paid vacations.

There are two very different types of freelancers. Those of the first type write whatever they please, then do their best to sell what they've written. These writers have a great deal of choice and control over what they write, but they tend to make far less money than other types of writers.

The other stripe of freelancer operates much like a craftsperson or consultant. They sell their services to organizations and individuals, and write whatever they're asked to write. They may bid on writing projects, or they may charge an hourly or daily rate. These writers tend to make considerably more money than the more self-directed type of freelancer, but they also have far less choice over what they write.

It is of course possible to work in more than one of these categories at once.

52

It's Possible to Get Rich by Writing—But It Doesn't Happen Often.

▪ ▪ ▪ ▪ ▪ ▪ ▪

We read in the newspaper about the writer who got a million-dollar advance for their first book, or who sold movie rights to their life story for $300,000, or who got $200,000 for the first screenplay they ever wrote. These stories are true.

They're also exceedingly rare. That's why they're in the newspaper. If they were common, they wouldn't be news.

It *is* possible to make hundreds of thousands, or even millions of dollars as a writer—but the odds are stacked heavily against it, even for those who do everything right.

There are really only four ways to become genuinely rich as a writer: 1) write a bestselling book (or at least one that earns a big advance); 2) write a hit movie (or one that sells for big money); 3) become famous, then write a book (or have someone ghostwrite it for you); and 4) marry someone famous, then write a book (or have it written for you). Options one and two are possible for perhaps one writer out of a thousand. Options three and four are far more unlikely still.

The fact is that no one really knows exactly what will sell and what won't. (If they did, every publisher and producer would be making scads of money.) No one expected Umberto Eco's *The Name of the Rose* to become anything like a bestseller—including Eco and his publisher. On the other extreme, HarperCollins printed 600,000 copies of Jay Leno's *Leading with My Chin*, and 400,000 copies came back to Harper unsold.

So what does make a writer rich? Luck, mostly, and persistence. The longer you keep writing and selling (or trying to sell) your work, the more you increase your chances of hitting the jackpot. But even if you plug away steadily for five decades, the odds are still something like fifteen to one against your ever becoming truly wealthy from your writing.

Occasionally you'll read about an author who decides to write a bestseller, sits down, writes a book, and, lo and behold, gets rich from it. (The two classic examples are *Love Story* and *Thinner Thighs in 30 Days*.) But what you won't read about are the many thousands of other writers who tried the same thing and failed. (After all, "Writer Publishes Book with Disappointing Sales" isn't news.)

So if you're looking to get rich, writing probably isn't the way to go.

On the other hand, there are quite a few ways to make an excellent living—i.e., $50,000 or more a year—as a writer:

- Write a Broadway show that runs a long time.

- Write a book, especially a textbook, that sells steadily and well.

- Write several books that all sell respectably and together earn a substantial sum in royalties each year.

- Write and sell material to the film industry on a regular basis.

- Write and sell projects for television on a regular basis.

- Get a job as a full-time staff writer for a magazine, newspaper, book publisher, or TV show.

- Get a full-time writing job outside of the media industries—e.g., as a corporate communications specialist, technical writer, advertising writer, public relations writer, publicist, etc.

- Become a full-time freelance writer, selling your services to businesses and nonprofits.

- Become a full-time contract writer, finding placements

through a contract placement service for forty to fifty weeks a year.

• Pursue some combination of the above.

But what about becoming a regular freelance writer for magazines and newspapers? Or regularly publishing books that sell in respectable but not huge numbers? After all, these are the two situations most beginners envision when they think, "I want to write for a living."

These are both worthy goals, but unfortunately there usually isn't a great deal of money in them. Full-time freelancers who write nothing but magazine and newspaper pieces earn, on average, between $15,000 and $25,000 a year—less than a secretary or a typist. Full-time book writers, unless they get lucky, typically earn about the same. (There are exceptions, of course. I have a colleague who makes nearly a six-figure income writing for magazines.)

If you want to write, great. If you want to get rich, that's fine, too. But if you want to achieve the second goal through the first, know that your chances of doing so are very slim.

53 There Is Far More Money in Writing for Businesses and Nonprofits Than There Is in Writing for Publication.

This may seem odd at first, since there are so very many publications out there to write for. But the need for writers goes well beyond what book, magazine, and newspaper publishers do. Hundreds of thousands of organizations—from Fortune 500 corporations to mom-and-pop businesses, from huge national nonprofits to local community groups—have an ongoing need for writers and editors. So do churches, retail shops, and virtually every type of governmental organization. And so do many individuals, from politicians to executives to professionals in all fields.

These people and organizations need literally billions of words written for them each year. They need speeches, press releases, brochures, instruction manuals, annual reports, in-house newsletters, video scripts, catalogs, flyers, business letters, memos, grant proposals, internal reports, and hundreds of other types of documents. They look to professional writers to create these documents for them—and usually they're willing to pay well, or very well, for those writers' services. (In Minneapolis, where I live, businesses and nonprofits pay freelance writers $40–$100 per hour.)

Most businesses and nonprofit organizations think of writers as white-collar professionals, much like consultants or attorneys, and usually treat them accordingly. They normally pay well and on time, give writers substantial respect, and appreciate their expertise. And because their need for writers is so huge, there are plenty of such opportunities to go around.

Writing for publication is a vastly different type of kettle filled with an entirely different species of fish. Because so many people want to be published, the competition among writers is enormous, particularly at high-profile publications. This drives standards up and rates of payment down; it also encourages many publications to refuse to deal with freelancers at all, and to work only with their own staff writers.

A writer can easily spend twenty-five hours writing a feature story for a magazine, and come away with $500 for her trouble. Or she can spend the same twenty-five hours writing an instruction manual for a software product, and earn $1,750. Which amount would you rather have?

Does this mean you should scuttle any dreams you may have of writing for publication, or making a living at it? Of course not. But it's important to know where the money is and isn't, where your chances for financial success are strongest, and where they are not as strong.

One option is to do what I do: write for businesses and non-profits, which is more lucrative, *and* for publication, which is more creative and fun. The result can be a satisfying balance of income and self-direction, stability and freedom.

Two excellent books on writing for businesses and nonprofits are:

- *Secrets of a Freelance Writer* by Robert W. Bly (Henry Holt)
- *Writing for the Corporate Market* by George Sorenson (Mid-List Press)

54
Plan to Start Out Small, Then Work Your Way Up Slowly.

No matter how good your work is or how talented you are, you are not likely to earn fame, recognition, or large amounts of money quickly. It usually takes years, and sometimes decades. Normally you'll have to build your career slowly, one step at a time.

Partly this is because most people will judge you by your credentials, experience, and connections rather than by your demonstrated ability as a writer. When you have few or no writing credentials, you'll often be ignored, turned away, or given only passing consideration.

But it also seems to be the case for more "cosmic" reasons. I'm no New Ager, so I say this with some trepidation, but some sort of karmic or energetic buildup does seem to occur as you put more time, effort, and energy into your writing career. Certainly you'll tend to become a better writer as time passes, but there's something else at work as well. Early on in your career, you can expend lots of energy, and either get nowhere or move very slowly. As time passes, though, it usually takes less and less effort to produce more and more results. (For an excellent, if fictionalized, example of how this mysterious process works, read Jack London's highly autobiographical novel, *Martin Eden*.)

So plan on building your writing career one step at a time. If you want to publish in well-known magazines and newspapers, don't send everything you write to the *New Yorker* and the *Chicago Tribune*. Start out with small, local publications. If you live in or near a big city, try the neighborhood paper or the suburban weeklies; if you live in a small town, talk to the editor of the town paper.

Or, if you prefer, write for some local special-interest publications (e.g., newsletters, magazines, and newspapers that focus on topics such as spirituality, Asian culture, food, gay and lesbian issues, etc.). Once you've published half a dozen or more pieces in these small markets, then and only then begin approaching large regional magazines and national special-interest publications (e.g., *Ski*, *American Hunter*, *The Artist's Magazine*, *Hadassah*, etc.). Then, once you've established a track record in these publications, partly shift your focus to getting your work to the *New Yorker*, *Harper's*, *Redbook*, *Architectural Digest*, and the like.

This step-by-step process seems to be particularly necessary for writers who wish to publish in major literary magazines. The editors at literary publications seem especially concerned with where you've published before and what credentials you've earned. Therefore, if you write poetry or serious fiction, you should expect to publish your first six to ten pieces in small, regional literary magazines before you begin approaching those with national readerships and reputations.

If your goal is a full-time writing job, don't expect to land a full-time journalist's position right off the bat (although this is sometimes possible at small-town and suburban newspapers, which pay extremely low salaries). Instead, plan to start out as a copy clerk, an editorial assistant, or a secretary to a writer or editor. Then work your way up steadily, one step at a time.

We all know of some exceptions to this stepping-stone principle. I've heard of a number of unpublished writers who have written pieces, sent them to the *New Yorker*, and quickly sold them for substantial sums. Writer Gretchen Kreuter, who previously had published very little in the popular press, wrote a book, sent it to only one editor—at Knopf—and was promptly offered a publication contract and a five-figure advance. Natalie Goldberg's first book of prose, *Writing Down the Bones*, became an instant hit, and went through over thirty printings in its first decade of life. Such examples are common enough that we've all heard a number of them—yet they're uncommon enough that they make the news.

How do you give yourself the chance to become one of the

lucky exceptions, without undermining the more important work of slowly, steadily, and patiently building your writing career? Simple: Follow the 90/10 rule. Spend 90 percent of your time and effort taking the steady, gradual approach, working to establish yourself solidly at one level before trying to move up to the next. But also spend about 10 percent of your time and energy on the long shots: the best-known magazines, the biggest book publishers, or the major producers. If you succeed, the strategy will pay off handsomely; if you fail, you've only lost a small investment of your time.

55

Most Communication Fields (Publishing, Film, TV, Etc.) Are Moderately to Highly Dysfunctional.

This is hardly news to anyone who works in one of these fields or deals with it on a regular basis. But it is a surprise to many beginners.

No industry is 100 percent sane and reasonable, of course. But some are more sane and reasonable than others. In my experience, on a scale of one to ten—with ten being total insanity and chaos—the film and TV industries rank a consistent nine, and the worlds of publishing and theater earn an equally consistent eight. None of this is likely to improve anytime soon.

It's not really important to understand why things are so crazy or how they got that way. But for your own sanity and happiness, it's important to be realistic about the people and organizations you may find yourself dealing with.

First of all, understand that most people in the media will probably treat you reasonably well most of the time. But don't be surprised if some of them do one or more of the following:

- Promise a response by a certain date, then miss that date by weeks or months—or never respond at all.

- Fail to return phone calls, or return them weeks late.

- Refuse to take your calls.

- Express great interest in your work, then send a form letter rejecting it—or, in some cases, never communicate with you again.

- Have an excellent and productive relationship with you, then suddenly—seemingly for no reason—become distant and cold, or stop communicating with you entirely.

- Act frantic, harried, distracted, exhausted, and overwhelmed most or all of the time.

- Try to end every phone conversation as quickly as possible.

- Promise to do something, then completely blow it off—and express no guilt, remorse, or concern about it at all.

- Become so paralyzed by micromanagement and office politics that they are unable to make any decision or take any action.

- Be perfectly friendly and cooperative until the issue of money comes up, then turn suddenly nasty and accusatory—and then become friendly again once the money discussion is over.

- Offer terms or fees that are unreasonably low or outright exploitive.

- Take months to make a decision or get approval on a project, then give you a week (or a day) to write it.

- Ignore your calls and letters for months, then suddenly call and say, "Can you do a piece for us on the topic of ___? I need your answer immediately."

- Accuse you of being unprofessional, when you've been both reasonable and fair.

- Become offended by a perfectly reasonable request.

- Pay writers late.

- Lose manuscripts, invoices, and other important documents.

- Ignore you and your work completely.

- Forget who you are.

It's essential that you not take these actions personally. If you do encounter them, remind yourself that 1) you probably aren't to blame for them (even if you're told that you are); 2) there probably wasn't anything you could have done to prevent them; 3) there may not be a way to avoid similar situations in the future; and 4) you're not the only one being treated badly by that person or organization. Above all, don't obsess about what happened. Simply remind yourself that you've been dealing with someone who works in a pretty crazy field.

Here are some other positive steps you can take:

- Remain polite, but also be firm and persistent when you know that your position is reasonable.

- If someone is a more than a week late in getting back to you, call them and politely ask for an update.

- Get the terms of any important agreement in writing. (Or, after you've made a clear oral agreement, send the other person a written list of the terms you've agreed to, along with a note saying, "Here's my understanding of what we agreed to. Please get back to me immediately if your understanding of our agreement is different in any way.")

- Go over people's heads when necessary. (Sometimes this is the only thing that works.)

- If a person or organization consistently treats you shabbily, simply stop dealing with them.

Exceptions to the general craziness abound, of course. There are plenty of people and companies in each of these fields that treat writers fairly and respectfully; that are honest, trustworthy, and reliable; that live up to their obligations and promises; that pay reasonably well and on time; and that operate sanely and humanely at least 90 percent of the time. But they are in the distinct minority.

56 Nonfiction Accounts for 95 Percent of All Published Material, and 95 Percent of All the Money Writers Make.

For every short story that's published, perhaps a hundred nonfiction pieces are published as well—in newspapers, newsletters, magazines, books, online publications, and a variety of other media. For every new novel that's released, book publishers release fifteen to twenty nonfiction titles—from memoirs to textbooks to auto repair manuals. And for every successful poet or scriptwriter in this country, there are probably forty or fifty successful writers of nonfiction.

Nonfiction also accounts for 99+ percent of all the *unpublished* material that writers get paid to create, such as speeches, reports, grant proposals, press releases, and so on.

If you're working on a novel, or a screenplay, or a musical, this doesn't mean you should stop. On the other hand, if your goal is to make money (or a living) as a writer, know that nonfiction is what publishers, businesses, and nonprofits most need—and are most willing to pay for.

57

There Are Three Ways to Publish Material in Periodicals:

1) Complete Whatever Pieces You Desire, Then Submit Them for Publication;
2) Pitch Ideas for Pieces to Editors, Then Contract in Advance to Write Them; and
3) Write Whatever Editors Ask You to Write, on Assignment.

■　　■　　■　　■　　■　　■　　■

A **periodical** (or **serial**) is simply a magazine, newspaper, or newsletter—something published periodically.

If you choose to submit a finished piece for publication, prepare your manuscript according to the samples on pages 141–43. Please note that prose and poetry require slightly different formats. In all cases, however, do the following:

- Use a standard, easy-to-read typeface such as Arial, Courier, Helvetica, or Times Roman.

- Use black ink or ribbon.

- Use a typewriter, word processor, or computer printer. Make sure the printing is dark and clear. Avoid dot-matrix printers unless they turn out text that's comparable to a good typewriter or ink-jet printer.

- Use white 8½-by-11-inch paper, without holes or lines. Computer or photocopying paper both work well; each is available for $2–$4 per ream (500 sheets). Avoid fancy papers such as onion skin or 100 percent cotton. (You may use cotton, linen, or laid paper for letters, however.)

- Print or type only on one side of each page, with margins of ¾ to 1 inch on all sides.

- Don't staple your manuscript; use a paper clip in the upper left-hand corner.

On top of your manuscript, also inside the paper clip, attach a letter introducing yourself and your work. (See the sample cover letter on page 144.) Don't give a sales pitch; that's considered both unnecessary and amateurish. Just describe the material in a phrase or two.

Be equally brief in discussing yourself and your credentials. Mention any relevant publications you may have, any awards you've received, and any relevant background or experience you may have (e.g., if your piece is about horse racing, mention that you were a jockey for three years). *Don't* mention anything that might be perceived as trivial, such as the pieces you published in your church newsletter or your honorable mention in the 1977 Nicollet Valley Community College poetry competition. Also don't mention any publications or credentials in a vastly different area—e.g., don't tell the editor at *Playboy* about your publications in the *Chronicle of Higher Education*, and vice versa. If you've got no credentials worth mentioning, then don't say anything about yourself at all.

Normally you should send only one manuscript at a time. If you are submitting short poetry, however, submit four to six poems at once, up to a total of about ten pages.

An alternative to submitting finished pieces is to pitch your idea to editors in the hope of getting an **assignment**. An assignment is a formal commitment between you and the publisher in which you agree to write a piece on a particular topic, and the publisher agrees to publish it. Unless little or no money is involved, you'll normally sign a formal agreement which specifies the piece's length, slant, and delivery date, as well as your fee and when it is to be paid (i.e., on acceptance, on publication, etc.).

Most assignment agreements also contain a provision for a **kill fee**. This is a percentage (usually 25–50 percent) of the originally agreed-upon payment. The editor has the right to choose not to publish your piece, return all rights to the piece to you, and pay you this kill fee. You then have the right to publish the piece anywhere else you please.

A sample letter pitching an idea and requesting an assignment appears on page 145; a sample assignment agreement appears on page 147. (Note the use of the editor's first name; publishing is, by and large, a first-name industry.)

Send in your pitch letter by mail or e-mail; if you use regular mail, enclose a self-addressed, stamped business envelope for the editor's reply. Follow up with a phone call if you haven't gotten a response after two weeks.

Important: Unless you are internationally famous, don't try to get an assignment to write a short story or poem on assignment. And until and unless you've published at least a handful of pieces, don't expect to land a nonfiction assignment from any but the smallest publications. (Remember, too, that those very small publications pay at most $50 per article, and many pay nothing at all.)

If you don't have much experience or many publications under your belt, one alternative you have is to pitch an idea for a piece, but agree to do it **on speculation** (or **on spec**). This is essentially a compromise between a standard assignment and a straightforward submission. If an editor has you write the piece on spec, it means they are seriously interested in publishing it, but do not promise to do so. No written contract or kill fee is involved. (Because you don't have much of a track record, they're not sure if you can write a publishable piece—so they don't want to take the risk of a formal assignment.)

Nevertheless, there are two significant benefits to writing a piece on spec. First, it's a way to get your foot in the door of a publication you haven't written for before. Second, if you need to gain access to hard-to-reach people (e.g., celebrities or politicians) or restricted places (e.g., those requiring a press pass or security clearance), writing something on spec will help you get that access. Imagine, for example, that you want to interview the mayor of Minneapolis. If your plan is to do the interview first and then try to find a publisher for it, you probably won't be granted an appointment with her. But if you can say, "I'm doing an interview for _____ magazine"—and you *can* say that if you're writing your piece on spec—then your chances of getting that interview increase enormously. (The mayor's assistant will probably call your editor to confirm your arrangement with the magazine—and of course the editor will say, "That's right; that writer is doing a piece for us.")

When you write for any publication for the first time, you may need to do that first piece on spec. Once that piece has been accepted for publication, however, you should expect to be able to write future pieces for that same publication on assignment.

If you have published at least half a dozen nonfiction pieces in respectable publications, you have yet another option. You can contact editors, send them samples of your published work, and offer to write anything they might need on assignment. A sample letter making such an offer appears on page 146.

Which route should you choose? Any one you prefer—or even all three. They're all legitimate, honorable, and potentially lucrative.

SAMPLE FIRST PAGE OF A PROSE MANUSCRIPT

Scott Edelstein
4445 Vincent Avenue South
Minneapolis, MN 55410
612-928-1922
612-928-3756, fax
scottedelstein@cpinternet.com

About 2800 words

YOUR TITLE GOES HERE

by Scott Edelstein

This is the accepted format for most prose manuscripts. Note that, except where otherwise indicated, all text is double-spaced.

Follow this template unless you are writing an essay intended for an academic or scholarly journal, in which case do the following things differently:

First, create and add a cover page. This will have your title and byline in the center. About three inches below your byline, type your name, address, phone number(s), fax number (if any), and e-mail address (if any). These items should be centered, and each should appear on a separate line (with your address taking up two lines). Single space all of these items. Your cover page will have no header, footer, or page number.

Your next page will be numbered page one, and will look exactly like page two of this sample prose manuscript, except that your piece will begin three or four double-spaced lines down the page. Subsequent pages will be identical to the sample of the following page.

SAMPLE SECOND PAGE OF A PROSE MANUSCRIPT

This is the form to use for subsequent pages of any prose manuscript, including one intended for a scholarly or academic journal. There should be a page number and a header in the upper right of each page. This should include either your last name, the title of the piece, or a key word or phrase from the title.

If you need to begin a new section, you may simply skip a line, like so:

Another option is to add a line of asterisks, which I'll do at the end of the following paragraph. To add emphasis, simply **bold**, *italicize*, or <u>underline</u> the appropriate words. (But pick a single option and stick with it throughout your piece.)

Unless the piece has been previously published, don't include a copyright notice or the words "all rights reserved"; these are unnecessary and look amateurish. Also don't include your social security number (you'll be asked for it at the appropriate time) or the rights you wish to sell (those will depend on where and in what formats the publication is distributed).

> *　　　*　　　*　　　*　　　*

It's fine to send editors clear photocopies, but make sure they are in good condition; shabby, dog-eared manuscripts announce to editors, "I've been rejected repeatedly."

Your manuscript should be as clean and error-free as possible. If you need to make a correction, it's best to run a new page rather than write in the correction by hand.

Your font may be 10, 12, or 14 point; 12 is most common. Experiment to learn what fonts are clear, attractive, and easy to read. (Some fonts look tiny in 10 point; others look just fine in that size.) Avoid fancy typefaces such as Script, Mistral, or Modern; keep your manuscript looking clear and simple. Don't gussy it up with borders, clip art, dingbats, your photo, or illustrations (unless they naturally accompany your piece).

SAMPLE POETRY MANUSCRIPT

Harriet Martinez Gold
566 Winsbury Avenue
Washington, DC 20009
202-555-5969

AS YOU CAN SEE

The format for a poetry manuscript
Is quite different from one for prose.

Your poem should be either single-spaced
(And double-spaced between stanzas)
Or one-and-a-half-spaced, with two and a half
Or three spaces between stanzas.

You may either type your poem flush against
The left-hand margin of the page or establish
A separate left margin for your text that
Centers the poem on the page, as I've done here.

If your poem continues onto the next page,
Simply place a header and a page number
In the upper right of the page, as in the prose
Manuscript sample on the previous page.

In the case of an overlong line, you can indicate
That the same line continues by indenting
          several spaces, as I've done here.

If the poem employs visual effects, such as
the unusual
                    placement of
                              words and lines,

    then feel free   to amend   this form as necessary.

SAMPLE COVER LETTER TO ACCOMPANY A MANUSCRIPT

92 Annapolis Lane
Eugene, OR 97402
541-555-0909

February 5, 1999

Ms. Eileen Clement
Hypothetical Review
2248 Wendell Road
Rochester, NY 14606

Dear Eileen Clement:

I've been writing short fiction for the past three years, and enjoying **Hypothetical Review** for the past five.

I'm pleased to send you my most recent short story, "The Woman Who Ran," which is based loosely on the life of one of the country's first female marathon runners. I've also enclosed the usual return envelope and return postage.

My earlier work has appeared, or is scheduled to appear, in **Upstate Review**, **New England Fiction Quarterly**, and **No Such Magazine**. I have an MFA from Hamline University and am currently at work on a novel.

Sincerely,

Mary Ann Jacobs

SAMPLE LETTER SUGGESTING AN ASSIGNMENT TOPIC

8 Harper Road
Omega, VA 22333
703-555-8660 (office); 703-555-9444 (home)
703-555-8850 (fax)
GWTicknor@hypo.com

February 2, 1999

Clara Hardwick
Employer Review
450 Product Court
Service, FL   33990

Dear Clara:

Every working day, American workers spend over 240,000 person-hours using water coolers. A recent study has shown that the average office worker spends seven minutes a day quenching their thirst. Multiply those seven minutes by a thousand or more employees, and these water breaks can make a real difference in productivity for large corporations.

Concern about this among management has sparked the development of a new product: the personal water cooler. Similar in design to an overlarge thermos, this inexpensive device keeps a gallon of water cold for up to ten hours. Placed near an employee's desk or work station, it can increase their productivity by reducing their number of trips down the hall.

Six manufacturers now produce and sell personal water coolers. Prices range from just under thirty dollars to just under fifty. Design, efficiency, and durability vary greatly.

I propose to prepare an article (tentatively titled "The Personal Oasis") of roughly 2500 words for **Employer Review** which will introduce these products, explain why they are useful, describe the features of each model, and rate each product for efficiency, convenience, safety, durability, and overall value.

My previous work has appeared in a dozen magazines, from **Glamour** and **Seventeen** to **National Business Review** and **Office Products Monthly**. In several of these magazine I've published pieces rating office products, including electric staplers, personal lighting, and telephone systems. My first book, **The World's Best Office Products**, is forthcoming from McGraw-Hill. Samples of my prior publications are enclosed.

If you're interested in assigning "The Personal Oasis"--or if you have any questions--please call or e-mail me.

Sincerely,

Grace Ticknor

Grace W. Ticknor

SAMPLE LETTER OFFERING TO WORK ON ASSIGNMENT

WILLMAR COMMUNICATIONS
233 Armitage Lane
Albuquerque, NM 87108
Phone: (505) 555-9221   Fax: (505) 555-9230   E-mail: WillmarCom@valis.com

---

March 1, 1999

Bert Carroll
Albuquerque Style
23 El Cholo Blvd.
Albuquerque, NM 87101

Dear Bert:

I've been enjoying *Albuquerque Style* since its first issue two years ago, and am pleased to see that it has achieved a wide readership throughout the state.

For the past four years, I've been writing freelance articles on assignment for a variety of magazines and newspapers, including *Parents*, the *Albuquerque Journal*, the *Denver Post*, *Organic Gardening*, *New Mexico*, *Southwest Profile*, and *Private Colleges*. Many of these pieces have dealt with people, places, institutions, and events in Albuquerque. I'll enclose photocopies of three such recent pieces.

I'm interested in doing some freelance work for you on assignment, and am open to virtually any topic dealing with Albuquerque or New Mexico. I work fast, do thorough research and interviews, and am scrupulous about meeting deadlines. As you'll see in the enclosed samples, I can modify my style to suit just about any topic or readership. I've lived in Albuquerque for the past eleven years, and wouldn't want to live anywhere else.

If this prospect interests you, please get in touch.

Sincerely,

Nan Willmar

Nan Willmar

The Imaginary Review
2100 Fantasy Road
Milwaukee, WI 53202
Phone: 414-555-2809   Fax: 414-555-2290
E-mail: ImagRev@aol.com

January 19, 1999

Kathryn Reed
88 Dayton Road
Cincinnati, OH   45220

Dear Kathryn:

I'm pleased to formally assign you the piece we discussed by phone earlier today, "Learning Made Memorable," for publication in **The Imaginary Review**. This letter outlines the terms we agreed to in our phone conversation.

The article will be about 2500 words long, and will introduce and explain the work of Dr. Marilyn Snyder, director of the Center for the Study of Cognition and Memory in Cincinnati. You agree to provide us with a copy of this article in finished form, both in hard copy and as a computer file in Word for Windows, on or before March 15, 1999.

In return, **The Imaginary Review** agrees to pay you $900 within 45 days of delivery and acceptance of the manuscript. This entitles **The Imaginary Review** to first world rights to the piece, in both print and online formats.

If we find your article unsatisfactory, we will provide you with clear guidelines for revision within 30 days of delivery, and you will get us a revised version no more than 30 days thereafter. If the revised manuscript is not acceptable, then we shall so notify you, at which point all rights to the piece revert to you. We shall also pay you a kill fee of $250 within 30 days, at which time both of us shall have no further obligation to each other.

Two copies of this letter are enclosed.   Please sign and date both copies, and return one to me.

I look forward to working with you on this project.

Sincerely,

Sheila Vilankulu
Senior Editor

I agree to the above terms: _____   Date:_____
                              Kathryn Reed

58

Unless You're Dealing with the Film or TV Industries, You Don't Have to Worry About People Stealing Your Work or Ideas. If You *Are* Dealing with Hollywood, There Is a Way to Protect Yourself and Your Work.

■   ■   ■   ■   ■   ■

Believe it or not, outside of Hollywood literary theft is actually quite rare. What little such theft there is takes two forms:

1. A publication reprints one of your already-published pieces without first getting your permission—and without paying you a fee. This does happen occasionally, though not often; when it does, the original writer's byline is usually included. Oddly enough, Christian publications seem to be the ones most likely to commit this sin.

2. Another writer takes your work, puts their name on it, and publishes it as their own. This is *extremely* rare; indeed, over the past twenty-five years, I have heard of only two such literary thieves.

But neither of these situations is what beginning writers fear most. Usually they're afraid that when they submit something to an editor, the editor will reject it, then give the basic idea to another writer—or even steal the idea themselves. Some beginners also worry about an editor making a copy of the piece, then publishing it themselves under their own name.

The reality is that both of these situations virtually never happen. In fact, I've not heard of a single case of either one over the past twenty-five years.

What does happen occasionally is that two different writers come up with the same idea, and both bring it to the same editor or publication. In such a case, the editor obviously can't say yes to both writers. Let's say they choose writer A, because A has better credentials and more experience. When writer B sees A's piece in the magazine a few months later, B is going to be understandably upset and suspicious. But is this theft? Hardly.

In any event, ideas are essentially public property. Individual literary works can be copyrighted, but ideas alone cannot be either copyrighted or trademarked. And that's the way things should be. If ideas *could* be copyrighted, public discourse would grind to a halt; the legal system would quickly become clogged with intellectual property lawsuits; and every publisher would close down out of fear of litigation. (Imagine this nightmare scenario: You're the editor of *Publishers Weekly*, and one day you get a semiliterate, nearly incoherent e-mail from an (obviously) unpublished writer, asking for an assignment to interview Stephen King. You say no, of course, but now you're forbidden from ever interviewing King, because that would be "stealing" the writer's idea.) Fortunately, that's not how things are.

If you want to make a movie about the sinking of the *Titanic*, that's perfectly okay, because "the *Titanic* sinks" is just an idea. But you *can't* use any of the characters or plot of the movie *Titanic* without the studio's permission, because, as essential parts of the film, they are protected by U.S. copyright law.

Which brings us to Hollywood—where, unfortunately, theft does occur considerably more often than in publishing (though only a tiny percentage of the time). Because the film and television industries are not paragons of trustworthiness, film writers' organizations have established services where, for a small fee, you can register your material before submitting it to producers. This registration clearly establishes your authorship and ownership. For more information on script registration, contact one of the following:

In the United States: The Writers Guild West, 7000 West 3rd Street, Los Angeles, CA 90048, 213-951-4000; or The Writers Guild East, 555 West 57th Street, Suite 1230, New York, NY 10019, 212-757-4360.

In Canada: The Writers Guild of Canada, 123 Edward Street, Suite 1225, Toronto, ON M5G 1E2, 416-979-7907.

Script registration is neither necessary nor recommended for audio, radio, or dramatic scripts.

59

You Don't Need to Register Your Work with the Copyright Office, or Mail a Copy to Yourself, or Print a Copyright Notice on It.

■　　■　　■　　■　　■　　■

Copyright law *automatically* protects anything you write *from the moment you create it*. You do *not* need to register it with the Copyright Office in order to obtain this legal protection.

Under U.S. law, copyright registration isn't necessary until your work is published or publicly performed—at which point the publisher or producer normally registers your work for you. (If a short piece you've written appears in a book or periodical, the copyright on that book or periodical automatically covers your piece as well.) So save your $20.

As for mailing a copy to yourself, this is utterly unnecessary. I don't know how this strange practice got started, but the idea behind it is that someone may steal your work, claim authorship, and be willing to go to court over the issue. To the best of my knowledge, such a thing has never occurred in the history of the United States. Anyway, to clearly establish authorship of anything you write, all you have to do is save your early drafts.

Lastly, printing a copyright notice on an unpublished or unproduced manuscript does not provide you with any more legal protection than the piece already has. You don't need to remind people that such protection exists, any more than you need to put a sign on your car that says "Stealing this car is a violation of the law." In any event, no one is going to look at your manuscript and think, "Aha! This foolish writer forgot to remind me that our country has copyright laws which protect their work. That means I can steal it!" (In fact, precisely because no such notice is necessary, writers who do put it on their work look amateurish to editors.)

There's an important caveat here, however. If your piece has already been published, then you *do* need to type or print a copyright notice on the first page. This keeps the copyright protection in force, and it alerts the editor to the piece's prior publication. (It's also a good idea to say in your cover letter when and where the piece was first published. This not only makes the piece's publication status crystal clear, but it emphasizes the fact that at least one of the editor's colleagues felt it was worthy of publication.)

60 Unless You Become Famous, Expect to Be Rejected Much or Most of the Time.

▪ ▪ ▪ ▪ ▪ ▪

If you're a runner, you don't expect to win every race. If you're a trial lawyer, you don't expect to win every case. And if you're single, you surely don't expect each new person you date to become your spouse. Why, then, should you expect all (or even most) of your writing efforts to be successful?

Actually, you have it better than the runner or the trial lawyer. When the lawyer loses in court, their client suffers. And when the runner loses a race, they can never rerun it. But if you're trying to publish a piece and it gets rejected, you can keep sending it around until someone says "yes" to it—and once you do have a "yes," it cancels out all the previous "no's."

Imagine that your memoir is rejected nineteen times, but on the twentieth submission you sell it for $10,000. It goes on to sell hundreds of thousands of copies, earn you half a million dollars, and win several awards. You *could* say that the book had a failure rate of 95 percent—but you'd be pretty foolish to think the book anything but a great success.

Don't think this is an impossible scenario. Robert Pirsig's *Zen and the Art of Motorcycle Maintenance*, one of the bestselling books of the twentieth century, was published by Morrow after receiving over 100 rejections. Richard Bach's bestselling *Jonathan Livingston Seagull* was rejected by eighteen publishers; Theodore "Dr. Seuss" Geisel's first book accumulated twenty-three rejections before finding a publisher. My own most recent book sold to a major publisher after nineteen rejections.

Of course, as you become a better writer and gain experience and credentials, rejection will probably become somewhat less frequent. But, except for the likes of Stephen King or John Grisham, it never goes away entirely. Although I ultimately publish almost everything I write, much of it still gets rejected—some of it many times—before it finds a home.

In fact, sometimes it makes sense to *increase* your rejection rate. For example, maybe you've established yourself as a writer for national special-interest publications, and you decide to make a concerted effort to break into high-profile magazines such as *Family Circle*, *Better Homes and Gardens*, and *Redbook*. As you focus more of your efforts on these magazines, your rejection rate is likely to skyrocket for a while, until you get your foot in some of these doors.

Granted, rejection never feels good—but you'll discover that, with experience, its sting becomes weaker and weaker.

In short, rejection isn't an evil to be eradicated, but a natural part of the writing business. So never take rejection personally, and don't assume it means your writing stinks. Instead, continue writing, selling yourself, and reminding yourself that persistence usually pays off.

The people who succeed in the writing business are the ones who don't take rejection very seriously, but who keep on patiently building their skills and their careers. Become one of these writers if you can.

It's Quite Simple to Establish a Pen Name for Yourself.

Pen names (or **pseudonyms**) don't need to be registered, applied for, or approved by anyone. Simply pick one and begin using it.

Look back at the sample first page of a prose manuscript, on page 141. Notice that the author's name appears twice: in the upper left-hand corner and near the middle of the page, directly beneath the title. If you want your piece to be published under a pen name, all you need to do is type it (instead of your real name) under the title. Editors will automatically understand that they should publish your piece pseudonymously—and that checks should be made out to your real name. (Leave your real name in the upper left for the benefit of editors and the people who cut checks.)

With poetry, the convention is a bit different. Put your real name in the upper left, as in the example on page 143; once the poem has been accepted for publication, drop the editor a note requesting that the poem be published under your pen name.

While you are free to choose any pen name you like, etiquette and common sense both dictate that you not use a name belonging to a well-known person—e.g., David Letterman, Tipper Gore, etc. D. B. Letterman would be fine, however.

If you want to adopt more than one pen name—one for your political commentary, perhaps, and another for your Westerns—that's fine.

If You're Serious About Marketing Your Writing, You Must Do Your Own Thorough Market Research.

■ ■ ■ ■ ■ ■ ■

Before a company puts any new product on the market, it does some market research to determine who the most likely buyers are. When you have a piece of writing that you hope to publish, you're in a similar situation. This means you need to do your own market research to determine which publishers, publications, or producers are most likely to be interested in what you have to offer.

One way to begin your research is to consult some market listings for writers. The best of these are:

Bacon's Magazine Directory (reference book, published annually). Lists many of the magazines published in North America, along with editors' names, positions, addresses, and phone numbers.

Bacon's Newspaper Directory (reference book, published annually). Provides a good list of newspapers of all sizes throughout North America, along with addresses, phone numbers, and editors' names.

Canadian Writer's Guide (reference book, published every other year). A good general reference covering Canadian markets.

Canadian Writer's Market (reference book, published annually). A guide to a wide range of Canadian markets for writers.

Children's Writer's and Illustrator's Market (reference book, published annually). A useful guide to a wide range of children's markets.

Directory of Literary Magazines (reference book, published annually). Quite helpful for poets and writers of literary fiction.

Dramatists Sourcebook (reference book, published annually). Probably the best market guide for playwrights.

Editor and Publisher International Year Book (reference book, published annually). A useful list of newspapers throughout North America and elsewhere, with addresses, phone numbers, and editors' names.

Freelance Writer's Report (newsletter, published monthly). CNW Publishing, Box A, North Stratford, NH 03590, 800-351-9278. A good source of general market information.

Hollywood Creative Directory (reference book, published each March, July, and November). A first-rate guide to Hollywood studios, production companies, and TV networks. The single best resource for writers of material for film and television.

Independent Publisher (magazine, published every other month). The Jenkins Group, 121 East Front Street, Suite 401, Traverse City, MI 49684, 616-933-0445. A good source of information on what many small- and medium-sized book publishers are publishing. The spring and fall "announcements" issues are especially useful.

International Directory of Little Magazines and Small Presses (reference book, published annually). Provides information on a wide variety of literary magazines and book publishers.

International Literary Market Place (reference book, published annually). A helpful list of book publishers outside of North America.

Library Journal (magazine, published once or twice a month, depending on the month). Cahners, 245 West 17th Street, New York, NY 10011, 800-523-9659. Through its articles, reviews, and ads, *LJ* provides a great deal of information on what hundreds of different book publishers are publishing. The spring, summer, and fall "new books" issues are especially helpful.

Literary Market Place (reference book, published annually). An excellent guide for writers hoping to publish their books. Contains information on a wide range of American and Canadian publishers, as well as book producers, literary agents, and other book publishing organizations and professionals.

Member Directory. Alliance of Resident Theatres/New York, 575 Eighth Avenue, Suite 175, New York, NY 10018, 212-989-5257. A listing of markets for plays in New York City.

New Media Directory (reference book, published annually). A useful directory of online and other new media markets.

Newsletters in Print (reference book, published every other year). An excellent source of information on a wide variety of newsletter markets.

Novel and Short Story Writer's Market (reference book, published annually). A useful and wide-ranging guide to markets for fiction.

Oxbridge Directory of Newsletters (reference book, published annually). A very good list of U.S. and Canadian newsletter markets.

Poet's Market (reference book, published annually). An excellent resource for poets looking to publish their work; covers both magazines and book publishers.

Poets & Writers (magazine, published every other month). Poets & Writers, 72 Spring Street, Suite 301, New York, NY 10012, 212-226-3586. Provides information on a wide variety of markets, but is particularly strong on literary magazines and literary presses.

Publishers Directory (reference book, published annually). A useful list of many book publishers, especially small, noncommercial ones.

Publishers Trade List Annual (reference book, published annually). An anthology of catalogs from a wide range of book publishers. Helpful for writers looking to publish their books.

Publishers Weekly (magazine, published weekly). Cahners, 245 West 17th Street, New York, NY 10011, 800-278-2991. This is the trade journal of the book publishing industry, and, thus, one of the best resources for writers seeking publishers for their books. The articles, reviews, and ads all provide lots of useful information. Particularly helpful are the spring, summer, and fall "announcements" issues, as well as the special issues highlighting children's books, religious books, business books, and other specialized areas of book publishing.

School Library Journal (magazine, published monthly). Cahners, 245 West 17th Street, New York, NY 10011, 800-456-9409. Through articles, reviews, and ads, *SLJ* provides helpful information on presses that publish books for children and young adults.

Small Press Review (magazine, published monthly). Provides a helpful look at what a variety of literary presses are publishing.

Songwriter's Market (reference book, published annually). The single best reference for songwriters.

Syndicate Directory (reference book, published every other year). A guide to newspaper and magazine syndicates that distribute columns and comics.

Theatre Directory (reference book, published annually). A useful list of markets for playwrights.

Theatre Profiles (reference book, published every other year). Theatre Communications Group, 255 Lexington Avenue, New York, NY 10017, 212-697-5230. Lists all the productions during the current or previous year for hundreds of theaters around the United States.

The Working Press of the Nation (reference book, published annually). Volume 1 provides a thorough list of newspapers throughout the United States, along with addresses, phone numbers, and editors' names. Volume 2 provides a similar list for magazines.

The Writer's Chronicle (magazine, published six times a year). Associated Writing Programs, George Mason University, Tallwood House, Mail Stop 1E3, Fairfax, VA 22030, 703-993-4301. A good source of information on literary magazines and presses.

Writer's Digest (magazine, published monthly). By far the best magazine for writers, and a helpful source of general (though not extensive) market information.

Writer's Guide to Book Editors, Publishers, and Literary Agents (reference book, published annually). The single best source of information on book publishers and the editors who work for them. Contains special sections on religious/spiritual and university presses. An invaluable resource for anyone who hopes to publish a book.

Writer's Market (reference book, published annually). A very large, and very informative, guide to markets of many different types, including book publishers (both North American and foreign), book producers, magazines, theaters, newspaper syndicates, film and TV producers, and greeting card publishers. Contains an excellent list of trade, technical, and professional journals.

Many of the above resources are also available on CD-ROM, on microfiche, and/or online.

Also helpful in getting you started are:

Genre newsletters (specialized newsletters covering specific genres and types of publishing), such as *Romantic Times* and *Locus*, a newsletter covering the science-fiction field.

Writers' centers' newsletters.

Another excellent way to begin identifying potential markets is to browse the relevant shelves of a very large library, bookstore, or newsstand (or, ideally, all three).

Market resources and browsing can only take you part of the way, however. Once you've come up with some potential markets, you need to examine each one more carefully, so that you know exactly what it is being offered to readers or audiences *right now*. This step is absolutely essential; without it, you may send your work to some marginal or inappropriate markets and miss out on some of the most promising ones.

Here's what to look at carefully in this final phase of your research:

For **potential magazine, newspaper, and newsletter markets:** Examine at least two recent issues of each publication, including the current one.

For **potential book markets:** Examine the current frontlist catalog for each publishing house. (A publisher's **frontlist** consists of the books it has just published and those it will publish in the four to six months to come.) These catalogs are usually available on request at no charge, though some publishers may charge you $2–$5, and a few will insist that you send them a nine-by-twelve-inch envelope and a dollar or two in postage. (For publishers' addresses and phone numbers, consult the Publishers volume of the reference work *Books in Print,* or its companion, *Forthcoming Books.* Both of these are widely available in libraries, in both print and CD-ROM form.) The newest "announcements" issue of *Publishers*

Weekly and/or the most recent "new books" issue of *Library Journal* will also provide you with a great deal of current, in-depth information.

For **potential dramatic markets:** Examine a schedule of productions for each theater's current or upcoming season. Most theaters will mail you a schedule on request at no charge. Also consult the reference book *Theatre Profiles*, described earlier in this chapter.

Important: Because each piece you wish to have published or produced is different, you may need to do separate market research for each one.

If all of this seems like a lot of work, you're right: It is. But most things worth doing require some hard work. In any case, what would you rather do: work hard and succeed, or do a half-hearted job and succeed far less often?

63

Use *Writer's Market* As One Place to Begin Your Market Research, but *Only* As a Beginning.

Writer's Market is the granddaddy of all resources for writers, as well as the bestselling writers' reference work in North America. This annual volume lists thousands of magazines, newspapers, book publishers, theaters, and other places where writers can sell their work. Published each September for the following year, *Writer's Market* is easy to find in libraries and bookstores, and is available in both book and CD-ROM form. Several related volumes are published each year as well: *Poet's Market* (in September), *Songwriter's Market* (in September), *Novel & Short Story Writer's Market* (in January), and *Children's Writer's and Illustrator's Market* (in January). A similar volume, *Canadian Writer's Market*, is published for markets in Canada.

If you've got material that you'd like to see published or produced, these guides are good places to begin your market research. Each listing contains an address, phone number, fax number, and e-mail address (if available); details on the types of material the market is looking for; and the name of a contact person. These listings can help you develop a pool of potential markets for just about anything you've written.

But this is only your first step. Venerable as *Writer's Market* may be, it simply cannot provide the kind of detailed, up-to-the-minute information you need in order to accurately assess any potential market. (The same is true of any other reference book for writers as well.)

Therefore, you *must* look more closely at each potential market you're considering. Again, this means examining current and recent copies of any magazines, newspapers, or newsletters you're thinking of sending your work to. If you have a play, it means ordering theaters' production schedules. If you want to publish a book, it means looking through publishers' catalogs, and reading the most recent "announcements" issue of *Publishers Weekly*, and/or the most recent "new books" issue of *Library Journal*. (In the case of a nonfiction book, it also means browsing bookstore and library shelves to find books that might compete with your own—and to examine those books carefully so that you can make your book different or better.)

Why is this second step so important? Because if you skip it, you will wind up sending your work to some highly inappropriate markets—and overlooking some extremely promising ones. That's because the information in *Writer's Market* isn't detailed enough to enable you to separate your best markets from the so-so ones—and from those that are long shots at best.

Unfortunately, this is where many beginning writers lose their way. Instead of completing the market research process, they rely solely on the listings in *Writer's Market*. As a result, all too often they wind up missing some great opportunities, pursuing some marginal ones, and in general wasting some of their time, energy, and money.

It's not that the people at *Writer's Market* are clumsy or sloppy; in fact, they're quite careful about accurately publishing the information they receive from publishers and producers. The problem is that the information they receive isn't always terribly accurate, detailed, or up to date. There are two reasons for this:

First, up to fifteen months can pass between the time a publisher provides information to *Writer's Market* and the time the edition it's published in is replaced by a new one. Nowadays, with so many publications changing their missions, finding new audiences, and changing or establishing new formats, the market that sounds perfect in *WM* may now be looking for entirely different kinds of material. (And even if that particular market hasn't changed, the contact person listed in *WM* might have been replaced with someone new.)

Second, the people who fill out and return *WM*'s questionnaires aren't always as careful or detailed as they ought to be.

Many markets simply list some of the general types of things they publish—how-to pieces, political pieces, fantasy, horror, lifestyle pieces, and so on—without saying much about what they focus on or who their readers are. For example, dozens of magazines say in *WM* that they publish personal experience pieces, but *Commonweal* (a magazine of public affairs, religion, and the arts) publishes a very different type of personal experience essay than *Good Housekeeping* does. Barron's and Butterworth-Heinemann both publish business books, but their books are meant to appeal to two very different groups of readers.

You should also know that the various *Writer's Market* volumes provide listings for only a portion—perhaps 35–40 percent—of all markets available to writers. The majority of book publishers, magazines, newspapers, newsletters, and theaters either fail to return their questionnaires to *WM*, aren't sent questionnaires in the first place (often the case with new or small markets), or ask *WM* not to list them.

Thus, if you rely solely on *WM* for market information, you may never learn about some of the very best markets for what you've written. This is precisely why it's so important to spend time browsing in large libraries, bookstores, and newsstands, and to consult the resources described in chapter 62 (page 155–60).

If you've got something you'd like to publish, do all your homework before sending it out. Start with *Writer's Market*—but then keep going. This extra effort will give your work its very best chance for success in the writer's marketplace.

64

Some of the Best-Paying Publications—And Some of the Easiest Ones to Get Published In—Can't Be Found at Any Bookstore or Newsstand.

■ ■ ■ ■ ■ ■ ■

These publications fall into three categories:

Trade magazines—magazines published for business owners, executives, managers, and other key people in particular fields and businesses. Virtually every area of business, no matter how seemingly mundane, has at least one trade magazine. Some examples: *Accounting Technology*, *HR News*, *Consultant Pharmacist*, *EMedia Professional*, *Corporate Meetings & Incentives*, and *Tow Times* (for the towing industry).

Medical publications—magazines written specifically for M.D.'s, such as *Hospital Practice*, *Medical Economics*, and *Physicians' Weekly*. Many other health care publications also pay very well, such as Mayo Clinic's *Mayo Online*, an Internet publication which presents 500-word articles for the general reader on a wide variety of medical topics.

Alumni magazines—magazines published by very large universities, highly selective smaller universities, and prestigious liberal arts colleges for their former students. (Alumni magazines published by other colleges and universities are often open to freelance writers as well, but they tend to pay less money.)

These publications are decidedly unglamorous, but most of them pay quite well—typically $800 to $1,500 for a short article. If prestige means little to you but being paid well means a lot, these are great publications to write for.

Because these publications are so obscure and unglamorous, their editors are often looking for writers—and they're frequently open to working with relatively new ones.

Close to 100 percent of the material in these magazines is

written on assignment, however, so you'll need to have published at least a handful of pieces in respectable publications before you approach any of their editors. You don't usually need a working knowledge of the field, though you do need a willingness to learn its basic lingo and concepts.

Because you can't find these publications in a bookstore, newsstand, or library, how do you get your hands on copies? In fact, how do you even find out what publications exist?

For trade and technical publications, start with *Writer's Market*, which lists many such publications and provides fairly detailed information on each one. Call up each magazine that sounds promising, explain to the operator that you're a freelance writer interested in writing for it, and ask to be sent a copy of the current issue. Sometimes you'll be sent one free of charge; sometimes you'll be asked to pay for a copy. Either way, you'll get your sample issue.

For alumni magazines, the process is even simpler: call the switchboard of the college or university and ask for the alumni magazine office; once you're connected, follow the procedure described above.

Incidentally, in publishing lingo **trade magazine** means "magazine not for general readers, but for people in a specific trade," while **trade book** means "book not for people in a specific trade, but for general readers." If you find that dichotomy bewildering and annoying, reread my comments in chapter 55 on the dysfunctionality of most communication fields (page 133–35).

65

It's Essential to Send Your Work Not Only to the Right Publishers, But to the Right Editors As Well.

■ ■ ■ ■ ■ ■

Imagine that you've received a package in the mail addressed to "Occupant" or "Current Resident." How interested would you be in opening it?

Now imagine that a second package arrives. This one is addressed to you by name, though you don't recognize the name of the sender.

Which of the two packages will you open first?

If you're an editor or producer, dozens of new manuscripts land on your desk every day. Which ones are you going to be more interested in reading: those addressed to you by name, or those addressed merely to "Editor" or "Fiction Editor" or "Production Department"?

If you're serious about getting published or produced, always send your work to editors and producers by name, not by title. If you don't, your work will probably be placed in what's called the **slush pile**—those manuscripts specifically earmarked to receive the least consideration. It may languish there for weeks or months, waiting to be read, while submissions addressed to the right people by name get read, carefully considered, and purchased. When your manuscript finally does get read, the reader may be a secretary or editorial assistant who has been told, "Just glance over each manuscript for a minute or so. Plan to reject pretty much everything, but if something does look promising, pass it on to an editor."

Actually, that's the *best-case* scenario. Many publishers and producers simply return pieces addressed to "Editor" or "Producer" to their senders without even looking at them.

Why set yourself up for such poor treatment, when you can avoid it simply by writing to someone by name?

"Wait a minute," you may be thinking. "In *Writer's Market* and other market listings, I often see the phrase 'Contact Editorial Department' or 'Send work to Manuscript Editor' or 'Direct all submissions to Acquisitions.' Shouldn't I follow these guidelines?"

No, you shouldn't if you want to keep your work out of the slush pile. In fact, one of the very purposes of many market listings is to separate the professionals from the amateurs—and professional writers know (just as you now know) that they've always got to approach editors by name.

As with just about everything else in the writing business, there are some exceptions—two, in this case. If you are either applying for a writer's grant or entering a literary contest, then sending your work to a specific person is neither necessary nor helpful, because your work will normally be reviewed by a panel rather than a single editor.

Because it is important to write to editors and producers by name, you need to determine who the right person is at any particular publisher, theater, or production company. But how do you find out who this person is?

You can, of course, always call up any publisher or producer and say, "I've written a [travel article, science fiction novel, memoir, film script, book review, one-act play, opinion piece, etc.] that I'd like to send your way. Who would be the best person to address it to?" In fact, that's exactly what you *should* do for the following media, since you'll probably get a direct, honest answer:

- newsletters
- newspapers (except for the largest and best known—e.g., *The New York Times*, *The Washington Post*, *The Wall Street Journal*, *USA Today*, etc.)
- syndicates
- small magazines
- small- and medium-sized theaters
- small film or TV production companies

- greeting card publishers
- very small book publishers

I would not, however, make such a call to a media organization that doesn't fit one of these categories, because you'll probably get told one of three things: 1) "Send it to the Editorial Department" (which you already know never to do); 2) "Send it to _____" (who will turn out to be keeper of the slush pile); or 3) "Don't send it at all; we don't read any unsolicited material, or material not submitted by a literary agent" (which is often untrue). Instead, you'll need to do a little research. Here's what to do:

BOOK PUBLISHERS

Consult the excellent reference volume *Writer's Guide to Book Editors, Publishers, and Literary Agents* by Jeff Herman (Prima), which is widely available in libraries and bookstores. Be sure to use the current volume, which is published in September.

Herman's book describes hundreds of different U.S. book publishers in some detail. It discusses their missions, needs, and **backlists** (books they've previously published), and lists the names of each company's **acquisitions editors**—those editors who review manuscripts for publication. Better yet, it describes the interests, mission, and focus of each editor. Herman's book also includes a guide to religious and spiritual book publishers (and their editors), as well as a guide to university and academic presses and editors. *Please note*: to locate publishers, use the index.

If Herman's book does not list a publisher you're interested in, then check *both* of the following:

Literary Market Place. This two-volume work is available in many large libraries. *LMP* is published in October, and it lists thousands of U.S. and Canadian publishers of all sizes, as well as a number of small presses. It usually says relatively little about each publisher, however, and even less about each editor.

Writer's Market. This book, which is easy to find in both libraries and bookstores, is published every September. It offers more information about editors than *LMP*, but less than Herman's book. WM also has supplementary lists of small presses and book publishers outside the United States.

Other potential sources of book editors' names and preferences:

Canadian Writer's Market
Children's Writer's and Illustrator's Market
International Directory of Little Magazines and Small Presses
International Literary Market Place
Novel and Short Story Writer's Market
Poet's Market
Publishers Directory

Because each of these resources is published only once a year, and because people in book publishing tend to change jobs with great frequency, you'll need to double-check whatever information on editors you find. I *strongly* suggest calling each press just before you submit your work and asking, "Is [name of editor] still with the company?" If that person's gone, ask, "Can you tell me who's currently acquiring books in that area?"

LARGE MAGAZINES

1. Check a current or very recent issue. Somewhere in the front, usually within ten pages of the table of contents, will probably be a list of key staff members, including editors.

2. Check one or more of the following annual reference books, all available in large libraries:

Bacon's Magazine Directory
Canadian Writer's Market
Children's Writer's and Illustrator's Market
Directory of Little Magazines
International Directory of Little Magazines and Small Presses
Novel and Short Story Writer's Market
Poet's Market
Working Press of the Nation, The, volume 2

Always pick the proper department editor (e.g., lifestyles, fashion, fiction, poetry, book reviews, etc.)—or, at very large magazines such as *Playboy*, *Redbook*, or *Vogue*, an assistant or associate department editor. At large magazines which do not have department editors (e.g., *Harper's*, *Atlantic Monthly*, etc.), send your work to an associate editor, senior editor, or assistant editor.

If you obtain an editor's name from a reference book, it is an excellent idea to call the publication and ask, "Is [name of editor] still with the company?" If that person's gone, ask, "Can you tell me who's currently handling material in that area?"

VERY LARGE NEWSPAPERS

1. Check a current or recent issue. Many newspapers print the names of section editors on the first or second page of each section; others list many of their editors on the editorial page.

2. Consult one or more of the following annual reference books, all available in large libraries:

Bacon's Newspaper Directory
Editor and Publisher International Yearbook
Working Press of the Nation, The, volume 1

If you use one of these reference books, I suggest calling each newspaper where you intend to submit your work, to make sure the editor in question is still there—and, if that person's gone, to learn the name of their replacement.

Keep in mind that your piece may be appropriate for more than one editor at any one newspaper—for example, your opinion piece on airline travel might be appropriate for the editorial section, the travel section, or the Sunday magazine supplement. If one editor says no, try another.

If you obtain an editor's name from a reference book, call the newspaper and ask, "Is [name of editor] still with the company?" If that person's gone, ask, "Can you tell me who's currently in charge of that department?"

LARGE THEATERS

Consult any or all of the following resources; call to confirm that the producer is still with the theater.

Dramatists Sourcebook
Member List, Alliance of Resident Theatres
Theatre Directory

FILM, TELEVISION, AND VIDEO

Consult *Hollywood Creative Directory*; call to confirm that the producer is still with the company.

SONGS

Consult *Songwriter's Market*; call to confirm that the producer or editor is still with the company.

NEWSPAPER AND MAGAZINE SYNDICATES

Consult *Syndicate Directory*; call to confirm that the editor is still with the company.

66 You May Send the Same Manuscript to Many Different Editors at Once.

■ ■ ■ ■ ■ ■ ■

Many years ago, it was standard procedure to send a manuscript to only one editor or producer at a time. For the most part, that practice was abandoned decades ago. It is now the norm to send the same manuscript—or to pitch the same assignment idea—to many (dozens, if you like) different editors or producers at once. And you don't need to explain that other editors are looking at it; that's automatically assumed. (This practice is sometimes called **multiple submission** or **simultaneous submission**.)

However, there remain a few circumstances in which it is still considered bad form to send a piece to more than one editor or producer at a time. Here are the guidelines to follow:

- Don't submit the same piece to more than one academic or scholarly journal at once. Ditto for journals of medicine, business, and law that have academic leanings or affiliations. (But go ahead and include university-sponsored literary magazines in your multiple submissions.)

- Don't simultaneously send the same piece to two daily newspapers in the same metropolitan area. (Because newspaper editors are on very tight deadlines, they sometimes rush pieces into print very quickly, then call the author the next morning and say, "Thanks for the article. It's in today's paper. We'll have a check out to you soon.") You don't want two competing papers printing your piece simultaneously.

- Don't send the same piece to two different editors at the same newspaper at once.

- If you've written a piece on assignment or under contract for a publisher or producer, you should of course send the finished project only to the organization you agreed to write the piece for.

- If your contract with a book publisher requires you to give that publisher an exclusive look at a subsequent book or book proposal before showing it to any other publishing house, of course abide by these terms. (But do your best to remove such a stipulation from any publication contract in the first place.)

Unless one of these exceptions applies, feel free to send anything you write to as many places as you like at once.

Avoid Sending Query Letters to Editors, Publishers, and Producers.

■   ■   ■   ■   ■   ■

A **query** is a letter, fax, call, or e-mail that describes a writing project you've completed, then asks an editor, producer, or agent if they're willing to read it. This is quite different from a letter requesting a magazine or newspaper assignment, which urges an editor to pay you to write a piece for the publication. Unless you're writing to a literary agent seeking representation, there are virtually *no* good reasons to write a query letter.

Suppose you send an editor a query letter asking if they'll read your novel. If you're lucky, *and* the editor has the time to read and respond to your query, *and* they're intrigued by your letter, where does this leave you? *Exactly where you would be if you had simply sent them the manuscript without querying first—except that by now it's days or weeks later.* And if they're not intrigued—or too busy to read or respond to your letter—you're stopped cold.

At best the process of querying gains you nothing; at worst, it gets you rejected without even having your work read.

So just skip the whole querying process and simply send editors or producers your manuscript. If you pick the right ones and send your work to them by name, chances are excellent that they'll open the package and read your work.

"But wait!" you may be thinking. "What about all those market notices in writers' publications that say 'query first' or 'no unsolicited manuscripts'? Shouldn't I take them seriously?"

No, you shouldn't.

You'll recall from chapter 65 (page 166–171) that publishers and producers try to welcome talented professionals while keeping amateurs at a distance. When they say "query first" and "no unsolicited manuscripts," pay no attention; they're simply trying to screen out the riffraff. Ninety percent of the time you'll get a reading, no matter what you're told in writers' resources.

Perhaps 10 percent of the time, however, editors and producers do mean what they say, in which case you'll get your manuscript back unread. But so what? It's a small loss to suffer in exchange for being read and taken seriously 90 percent of the time. (In any event, if a manuscript does come back with a note telling you to query first, you can *then* go ahead and query the editor or producer about it.)

After all of this query-bashing, you may be surprised to learn that in one circumstance a query is normally an excellent idea: when you approach literary agents in the hope of obtaining representation.

Why does querying make sense for agents but not for publishers and producers? For the simple reason that 90 percent of editors and producers will read your unsolicited manuscript, no matter what they may say publicly, but only about 40 percent of literary agents will. For details on approaching agents, turn to chapter 77 (page 191).

68 Most Editors and Producers Will Not Give You Much Feedback on Your Work.

▪ ▪ ▪ ▪ ▪ ▪

Providing feedback to writers isn't part of an editor's or producer's job. They're responsible for finding, acquiring, and editing manuscripts, not coaching freelancers. Most of the time you'll simply get a polite yes or no.

Even when you do get a yes, don't expect much in the way of comments or enthusiasm. Usually you'll get something like this: "Your piece looks good and we'd like to use it. We can offer $400. Shall I put a contract in the mail?"

Remember, editors and producers read and buy manuscripts all the time. To you, each writing deal is important and exciting; to editors and producers, it's just another part of their job.

Feel free to be as excited as you like, of course. Just don't expect the same enthusiasm from your editor or producer.

Some (though by no means all) book editors, play producers, and film producers—and even a very small number of magazine editors—are exceptions to this general rule. These editors and producers often provide useful and detailed feedback to writers, particularly those whose work they feel is close to meriting publication or production, but needs some shaping or polishing. These editors and producers can often be writers' most ardent supporters. It's a shame there aren't more of them.

When Editors and Producers *Do* Give You Feedback, Don't Take It Too Seriously Most of the Time.

Editors and producers tend to be overworked, frazzled, and pressed for time. As a result, what feedback they do provide is rarely carefully considered.

If an editor rejects your manuscript and makes specific comments on it, consider them entirely on their own merits. Don't give them extra weight because of who made them—in fact, considering the pressures that editors and producers typically work under, it's not a bad idea to take them with a little extra salt.

There are, however, two situations when you should take editors' and producers' comments *quite* seriously: 1) when they have accepted your work but suggest changes; and 2) when they like what you've written but want some revisions before they'll formally accept it.

In either case, you don't usually have to follow their suggestions to the letter. Most are open to some discussion and polite debate. Indeed, when a good writer and a good editor work together, the writer typically winds up taking about two-thirds of the editor's suggestions. The two of you should share the same ultimate goal: getting your piece into the best possible shape, and then getting it produced or into print.

70 Treat Editors, Producers, Agents, and Other Media Professionals Like Normal Human Beings.

■ ■ ■ ■ ■ ■

These people aren't gods, or tribal elders, or shamans, or dictators. They're just people with media jobs. And those jobs don't make them special in any way.

There's no need to be shy, or nervous, or humble, or arrogant, or excited, or unctuous, or pushy around them. Just be yourself.

Editors, publishers, producers, and agents may have the power to say yes or no to your writing, but that doesn't make them any better or more powerful than you. Treat them the same way you treat your mechanic, your dentist, and your accountant—as equals. Be honest, businesslike, fair, and forthright with them, and expect the same behavior in return.

It's probably too much to expect media people to regularly be polite and friendly, though. Since so many of them are frantic and stressed-out much of the time, they are likely to be very brusque, businesslike, fast-paced, and to the point.

It should go without saying that bribery, toadying, and sucking up not only are smarmy, but almost never work.

71

When an Unexpected Opportunity Arises, Don't Be Afraid to Grab It.

■   ■   ■   ■   ■   ■   ■

Maybe you're a nature writer, and suddenly you're offered the chance to edit a newsletter on thoroughbred horses. Or perhaps you're a novelist who is unexpectedly given the chance to move to Fiji and write for sailing magazines. Or maybe you're a full-time journalist for a big-city daily who gets offered a job as a staff writer for *Newsweek*.

When this kind of opportunity appears out of the blue, should you take it?

It depends. Ask yourself these questions:

- Do I have the ability, skills, and intelligence to take on this opportunity and be successful at it? (If the answer is no, proceed no further. But if it's yes or even maybe, continue with the questions below.)

- Does this opportunity excite or energize me?

- Does it scare me? (If so, acknowledge the fear, but don't base your decision on it.)

- What is the best thing that could happen if I take this opportunity? The worst? The most likely?

- What will probably happen if I *don't* take the opportunity? How do I feel about this?

- How satisfied am I with my current professional life? Would taking this new opportunity make me more satisfied, or less?

- Does the prospect *feel* right or wrong? (Ask your gut; it knows.)

Ultimately, the decision is yours alone. But here's a tip: As you make your decision, base it on growth, not on fear.

72

Virtually Everything in a Publishing Contract Is Potentially Negotiable.

Not everything in every contract is negotiable, but *some* of the terms in virtually every contract are.

Nevertheless, exactly what can and cannot be negotiated may differ enormously from one publisher to the next. One large newspaper may offer you $250 for your article and say, firmly but politely, "That's what we can offer; do we have a deal or not?" Another may offer $300, but be willing to go to $500 if pushed. A third may hold the line at its offer of $250, but say, "We'd be okay if you did 1,000 words for that price instead of the 1,500 you've suggested."

The book publisher Hypothetical House might refuse to negotiate on your **advance** (money paid to you up front) but be happy to negotiate on rights and **royalties** (earnings from sales of copies of the book). In contrast, Theoretical Press might be willing to triple its initial offer of an advance, but refuse to budge on its royalty rates. And Imaginary Books might be flexible on advance, royalties, rights, and a variety of other issues—but absolutely refuse to give you more than twenty-five free copies.

It's actually pretty rare to have to either take the precise terms you're offered or walk away. And it's rarer still for a legitimate publisher to pull out of a deal just because you asked for more. (In fact, if you do ask for better terms and the editor responds, "How dare you! The deal is off," something was surely fishy about the bargain in the first place.)

You might not get everything you ask for, of course—and once in a while you may not get *any* of it. But the worst you'll be told is, "Sorry, we can't do that."

None of this means that you *have* to ask for better terms. If you're happy with what you're offered, take it. But if it seems like too little, don't be afraid to ask for more.

Here are other important tips on negotiating a publishing contract:

- It's not uncommon for a publisher to mail you its "standard contract" (also known as its **boilerplate**), accompanied by a bland note that says, "Please sign and return." It will seem as if that's precisely what every other writer does. In fact, however, there is usually room to negotiate—often *lots* of room. (For example, if there's no mention of a fee—or, in the case of a book, no mention of an advance—ask for one; there's a good chance you'll get it.) I recently received a contract (and a "please sign and return" letter) from a large medical publisher asking to reprint a 400-word book excerpt in two of its annual reference books. No money was mentioned, so I called the person who had written the letter and asked for $300. She said "That's fine" so quickly that I suspect I could have gotten quite a bit more.

- Be willing to trade and compromise. If you're offered $250 for a 2,000-word feature article on aging and you'd like $500, by all means ask for $500—but be willing to settle for $350. Alternatively, offer to throw in a 500-word sidebar on nursing homes for a total of $400. Or agree to do 1,500 words for $250, and explain that you'll want a slightly higher rate next time.

- Don't ask for the moon. If you're offered $200 for your short story, don't ask for $1,500, or even $1,000, because no publication has a budget that flexible. But if you start by asking for $300–$500, there's a good chance that you can work out a compromise. (To learn what rates a particular publication pays, consult *Writer's Market*.) Keep in mind that the more publications, experience, and credentials you have, the more money and better terms you can usually expect.

- Unless you've been offered a contract for a book, or for TV, film, video, or major theatrical production, don't anticipate extended negotiations. Expect to agree on final terms very quickly—usually in thirty seconds to three minutes.

- If you *have* been offered a contract for a book—or for TV, film, video, or major theatrical production—one option you have is to hire a professional to negotiate it for you on a fee-for-service basis. Your options here include a literary agent, a literary consultant with a background in contract negotiation, or a publication lawyer. (Use the resources listed in chapter 77 (page 191–95) to locate one or more of these professionals.)

- Contract negotiation is an art, not a science. Some people are naturally better at it than others, though most people can learn it over time. It's usually difficult for beginners, however, so expect to make mistakes, especially in your first few deals. Be patient with yourself. With practice, you'll get better and better at it.

For more detailed information on negotiating a publication contract, consult one of these books:

- *Writer's Guide to Contract Negotiation, A* by Richard Balkin (Writer's Digest Books)

- *Indispensable Writer's Guide, The* by Scott Edelstein (HarperCollins)

- *1,818 Ways to Write Better and Get Published* by Scott Edelstein (Writer's Digest Books)

- *Negotiating a Book Contract* by Mark L. Levine (Moyer Bell)

73
Don't Be Afraid to Ask for What You Want or Need.

■ ■ ■ ■ ■ ■

This applies not just to contracts, but to any situation you encounter as a writer.

If someone you're interviewing isn't being clear, ask them to explain or provide clarification. If an editor says they want your piece by February 19 and you genuinely need until March 1, say so—and stick to your guns. If you feel some of the editing on your book was botched, change the text back to the original on your page proofs. Stand up for what you feel is necessary or important.

At the same time, be aware of the difference between what you want and what you need. If you're negotiating on something you *want*, be prepared to compromise, and even to take no for an answer. But if it's something you *need*, be willing to walk away if you can't come to an agreement.

The trick is to avoid being exploited—and also to avoid being arrogant.

74
Don't Promise Anything You Can't Deliver.

▪   ▪   ▪   ▪   ▪   ▪   ▪

Editors and producers are notorious for asking for the impossible and the nearly impossible. "I need a 4,000-word piece on Prince Charles by tomorrow morning." "We need the completed book in three months." "We'd like you to be part of this project, but we have to have all materials in hand by a week from Friday." "I know the deadline is awfully tight, but our company has a reputation for working miracles."

If you're offered this sort of high-pressure writing assignment, *don't* make a snap decision on it, no matter how much you may want the deal—and no matter how hard you're being pushed to decide quickly. You need to consider the offer thoughtfully and carefully, because you don't want to make a promise you'll regret.

Begin by looking at the situation as honestly and objectively as you can. Are you being asked to do something that's simply impossible for you? If so, don't say yes to it. *Under no circumstances agree to do the impossible*, because if you do, you'll fail—and you'll be held 100 percent responsible for that failure.

Instead of saying yes, you have three options: 1) say no; 2) offer to complete a scaled-down version by the deadline; or 3) offer to complete the full project by a later deadline.

If you're told, "Sorry, I can't play with deadlines or shorten the project; I absolutely have to have it all by that date," then your only sane response is, "I'm sorry, but if that's really the case, I suppose we can't work together on this project." (Here's a variation you can use that's very effective: "Well, we've got two options here. I can promise it to you by May 19 and deliver it by June 1, or I can promise it by June 1 and deliver it by June 1. Which would you prefer?") As you'll discover, half the time the other person will back down and say, "Oh, all right, we'll extend the deadline."

What if you *can* do the project by the deadline, but know it will require long hours, some rearranging of your schedule, and the patience and support of your family? Then ask yourself this question: *Is what I'll get out of it worth the stress, the disruption, and the long hours?*

If the answer is yes, then take the assignment and get cracking. But if the answer is no, then figure out what you *would* need to make the deal worthwhile. Ask for this, even if it seems exorbitant. You might get it.

If you don't get what you ask for, walk away. But if you do get it, roll up your sleeves and begin.

The principle of not promising more than you can deliver also applies to less high-pressure situations. For instance, if you contract to write a book, add an extra three months to your deadline to allow for illness, emergencies, and surprises. If you're accepting a magazine assignment, build in an extra couple of weeks of slack for the same reason. Plan for the unexpected, so that you always deliver everything you promise with a minimum of stress—and with time to spare.

75 Most Published Nonfiction Books Start Out As Book Proposals.

▪   ▪   ▪   ▪   ▪   ▪   ▪

There are two ways to present a nonfiction book to editors: as a finished manuscript or as a **book proposal**—a document that describes the book you wish to write. (Either one should be accompanied by a brief cover letter, of course, as per the example on page 144.)

A proposal gives editors (and their colleagues in the marketing, sales, and rights departments) a clear sense of your book's structure, tone, contents, intended readership, and sales potential. Typically, a book proposal contains a cover page; a one- to five-paragraph biography of the author; one or more sample chapters (however many are necessary to give a clear sense of the book's style and flavor); an introduction (if appropriate); a table of contents; an outline of the entire book; and a project overview.

The overview is in many ways the most important part of the proposal, because it is what editors use to generate enthusiasm for your book among their colleagues. Your project overview can take any reasonable form, but it should normally contain the following information:

- Who will buy the book.

- What benefits the book will provide for the reader.

- Why the book is necessary or important.

- How and why the book is better than (or at least different from) anything else currently available on the subject.

- Your credentials: why you have the authority, experience, or background to write the book.

- A list of four to six competing books (including titles, authors, publishers, and publication dates), with a very brief explanation of what each one lacks or why it is inferior to your book.

- Suggestions for how and where the book can be sold (optional).

- What you will do to help promote, publicize, and sell the book (optional).

Not all nonfiction books lend themselves well to the proposal form. If you have a memoir, for example, a proposal isn't likely to do it justice unless it's got a very juicy plot or some famous people as characters. If you're writing a memoir, it's usually best to finish it before trying to find a publisher for it.

I also wouldn't write a proposal for any very short book—e.g., a children's picture book. It makes little sense to propose to write a book that you can complete in a relatively short time.

It should go without saying that if you've already finished your book, there's no point in creating a proposal for it; simply submit (or have an agent submit) the completed manuscript.

Editors at all the large book publishers and most of the medium-sized ones are happy to consider nonfiction proposals. Some of the smaller presses, however, never offer writers contracts based on proposals, but must always have a full manuscript in hand in order to make a final decision.

Novels can sometimes be sold via proposals, but not if they're written by beginners. In general, you'll need to have published at least one novel, or at least two or three books (e.g., a memoir and a collection of short stories) in order to go the proposal route for a novel.

There are some notable exceptions, though. If you've published a dozen or more short pieces in a particular subgenre—e.g., mystery, romance, science fiction, or horror—then you've got a decent chance of selling a novel in that same subgenre via a proposal, even if you haven't published a book before. The same is true if you've published quite a few pieces for young adult readers (ages eleven to sixteen) and have a proposal for a young adult novel.

Short story collections and books of poetry are virtually never sold via proposals.

For more details on preparing a nonfiction book proposal, consult one or more of these books:

- *1,818 Ways to Write Better and Get Published* by Scott Edelstein (Writer's Digest Books)

- *Write the Perfect Book Proposal: 10 Proposals That Sold and Why* by Jeff Herman and Deborah Adams (Wiley)

- *How to Write a Book Proposal* by Michael Larsen (Writer's Digest Books)

Detailed information on creating a proposal for a novel appears in *Manuscript Submission* by Scott Edelstein (Writer's Digest Books).

76 You Don't Need a Literary Agent Unless You Wish to Sell a Book, a Full-Length Play, or Material for Major TV or Film Production.

◼ ◼ ◼ ◼ ◼ ◼

In fact, unless you're already a celebrity, you normally you can't *get* an agent to represent anything else. There's simply not enough money in it for the agent. However, a small number of agents do represent columns, comics, and other material for national syndication; a handful represent computer software products; and a few represent scripts for video.

It's usually tough (though sometimes possible) to get an agent if you've written a reference book, a literary novel, a short story collection, a textbook, a picture book for small children, or any book for a strictly limited audience. And if you have a poetry book, your chances of getting an agent for it are virtually zero— unless you're already famous or the book is extremely unusual in some way.

So if necessary, take a deep breath, roll up your sleeves, and start marketing your work yourself. Follow the guidelines in chapters 62–67 (pages 155–75), 72–73 (pages 181–84), and 75 (page 187–89).

To Get an Agent, Write a Brief Letter to Twenty to Twenty-Five People Selected from the Resources Listed in This Chapter.

All of the following resources contain good lists of literary agents. They are listed in order of usefulness.

Writer's Guide to Book Editors, Publishers, and Literary Agents by Jeff Herman (Prima). Published annually in September (the 2000–01 edition will be published in late 1999). Available in many libraries and bookstores—and, at under $30, quite affordable. Contains very detailed information on a fair number of agents, including their likes, dislikes, specialties, backgrounds, and recent sales. This book focuses primarily but not entirely on book agents.

Guide to Literary Agents edited by Donya Dickerson (Writer's Digest Books). Published annually in January. Widely available in bookstores and libraries. Includes detailed information on many agents, including each one's interests, specialties, credentials, and recent sales. Includes a good list of agents who handle material for film, television, and stage.

Literary Market Place (Reed Elsevier). Published annually in October. Available in many large and midsize libraries, usually in the reference section; not available in bookstores (and, at a price of $200+, not worth buying). Includes less detailed information than the above volumes, but lists many more agents. Covers agents of all types.

The National Writers Union (113 University Place, 6th Floor, New York, NY 10003, 212-254-0279) maintains an online database describing a variety of book agents. Although it profiles a smaller number of agents than any of the other resources, it rates each agent based on members' experiences. This guide is available only to NWU members; however, virtually all writers may join the organization, including those who have not yet had any work published or produced.

Hollywood Agents and Managers Directory (HCD). Published each February and October. Contains a list of 1200 film and TV agents and managers, including literary agents who handle television and film material.

While some agents are happy to read unsolicited manuscripts, most are not. Therefore, the best way to begin approaching agents is by sending a query letter. (Most agents prefer a regular letter to a fax, phone call, or e-mail message.)

Getting an agent usually involves playing the percentages, so it's important that you write to at least twenty agents at a time. (Typically, if you're an unpublished or unproduced writer with a good, salable writing project who writes to twenty agents at once, four or five of them will ask to see it; thirteen or fourteen will say no; and the remaining ones won't respond at all. Of the four or five that ask to see it, one or two will offer representation.) Write a separate letter to each agent, of course, though it's fine to use the same basic letter and simply change names and addresses. Address agents by their first names ("Dear Julienne"), since it's a first-name industry.

Your letter should be no more than one to two single-spaced pages. Begin by introducing yourself and your writing experience in one or two sentences. (If you have no significant publications or qualifications, omit this paragraph.)

Use your next two to six paragraphs to describe your writing project in detail. Begin by indicating whether the project is a finished book, a book proposal, a film treatment, a full-length play, etc. Then proceed as follows:

For nonfiction books, discuss your project's theme, approach, audience, purpose, and content.

For any other type of project, write a very brief plot synopsis. This should focus strictly on the action that occurs in the piece—not on themes, motivations, metaphors, or your intentions as a writer. Use third-person, present-tense language (for a memoir, use first person).

LETTER TO AGENTS ABOUT A NOVEL

Agent Name
Address
Address

August 9, 1984

Dear (first name):

I am a mystery writer who has sold five stories to **Hitchcock's Mystery Magazine** in the past eighteen months. The first of these stories appeared in the March 1983 issue; the last is not yet in print.

Two of the stories involve the hero of a murder mystery I have written, entitled **MURDER AT THE WAR**. The novel is traditional in structure and set in an "exotic locale"--a simulated medieval war. Every year 3000-plus members of the Society for the Advancement of Medievalism gather at a campground in western Pennsylvania to hold a mock war. Everyone dresses in medieval garb (including steel armor for the fighters), and the campground joyously drops out of the twentieth century for a three-day weekend.

During the course of a mock battle in the woods, however, a man is found dead--really dead, not mock dead. The woman who finds him becomes the chief suspect. She also happens to be the wife of Peter Brichter, a police detective from out of state.

The local law enforcement officers are startled at the sight of all these oddly-dressed people, and half-convinced they are some kind of cult. Brichter, trying to clear his wife, begins his own unofficial investigation, but the local police angrily call a halt to his activities and confine him to his encampment.

Meanwhile, the clues lead to a certain Lord Christopher, who, dressed in armor, participated in a mock skirmish beside the victim shortly before the murder. Lord Christopher's armor is found abandoned in the woods near the body, and it seems that no one had seen or heard of him before he appeared in the woods, dressed for battle. All of this suggests that there is, in fact, no Lord Christopher--that he was a SAM member who assumed that persona (and armor) as a disguise only for a few minutes, for the specific purpose of killing his victim and then escaping detection. There were 200 participants in the woods battle; any of them might have slipped away for a brief time.

While the local police struggle with the esoterica of the Society, Brichter welcomes visitors into his tent, fitting the pieces together in classic detective style.

There really is a medievalist society which holds an annual mock war in Pennsylvania. I am a member, and drew on my experiences at several of these wars in writing this book.

The novel is now in finished form, about 90,000 words long. Please let me know if you would be interested in reading it with an eye toward representing it.

Sincerely,

Mary Kuhfeld

LETTER TO AGENTS ABOUT A NONFICTION BOOK

September 11, 1997

Agent Name
Address
Address

Dear (first name):

You may have read about me in one of many magazine or newspaper features, or seen me on TV. I'm an ex-drug kingpin, gang leader, street kid, burglary ringleader, and convicted felon. Twelve years ago, however, I turned my life 180 degrees around, and over the past decade have run several profitable--and very legal--businesses. Currently I'm president of a successful company, Spinoza, which markets an unusual teddy bear. I also lead workshops on personal growth and accountability, am a frequent speaker in the public schools, and have been featured frequently in the media.

I've just finished a proposal for a book that may help to reduce crime, strengthen our economy, and change a great many people's lives for the better. The book, **How to Be a Successful Criminal: A Survival Guide for Kids**, speaks directly to anyone contemplating--or already living--a life of crime. In very straightforward, in-your-face language, it demonstrates clearly why most crimes are risky, low-return ventures which are likely to lead to jail, injury, or death. Next it shows that the very same skills a successful criminal needs can be used to run successful, low-risk, legitimate, one- and two-person businesses. Then **How to Become a Successful Criminal** demonstrates to young people, step by step, exactly **how** to make decent money in this dangerous world while keeping themselves safe, off drugs, and away from crime.

How to Be a Successful Criminal helps young people see that they have choices beyond the drudgery of corporate servitude and the potentially deadly realities of crime. More importantly, though, it helps people learn **how** to transfer "criminal" skills to ventures that enable them to live in the straight world without having to sell their souls to it.

My target audience is young males, ages 12-20--the segment of our society most likely to turn to crime. However, the book is also written to appeal to both younger kids (ages 7-11) and young adults in their twenties. I'm very familiar with these groups for two reasons: first, because I am a frequent and widely-sought-after speaker in schools, bringing the message behind **How to Be a Successful Criminal** to kids through short talks that I give throughout the Midwest; and, second, because the approach, design, and language of the book are the result of market testing with six focus groups of kids aged 13-18 in the past months. (I've also run the project past many social workers, counselors, and other professionals who work with at-risk kids. As a result, I've obtained a number of strong endorsements which can be used to help promote the project.)

While sales made directly to this target audience should be significant, the strongest potential for sales will be to parents; school and public libraries; teachers; guidance counselors; school administrators; psychologists and social workers; law enforcement professionals; corrections professionals (probation officers, parole officers, etc.); and community service professionals and groups. (I should add that I know the school market well, having sold 17,000 copies of another title in the past 18 months through schools in Minnesota and Colorado.)

You've been recommended to me as an experienced and able agent who would do a good job in helping this important project find the right home. If you'd like to see the proposal for **How to Be a Successful Criminal**, please give me a call, or drop me a note in the enclosed SASE.

Sincerely,

Ron Glodoski

If you prefer, you may drop the description or synopsis from your letter and attach a longer version as a separate document. This should run two to eight double-spaced (or one-and-a-half-spaced) pages. Refer the agent to this document in your letter.

In the paragraph that follows, discuss your credentials and publications in more detail. Include any information that might impress the agent, including any experience that may be relevant to your project. (If you have few or no such credentials, omit this paragraph.)

In your final paragraph, ask the agent if they would like to see the manuscript. Enclose a self-addressed, stamped business envelope. Send your letter via regular mail.

Two sample letters to agents can be found on pages 193–94. This first describes a mystery novel which was ultimately published by St. Martin's Press, then reprinted by Berkley as *Knightfall*. (Its author has since gone on to publish over a dozen novels and many more short stories.) The second is for a nonfiction book which was taken on by an agent and published in 1998.

Important: Do not send these letters until you have a project 100 percent ready for an agent to look at. There's no point in generating interest, only to have nothing to send.

If you get no bites after the first round of twenty to twenty-five letters, by all means send out another batch. In fact, I strongly suggest that you keep trying until you either get an agent or have accumulated at least one hundred refusals.

For more details on getting and working with a literary agent, consult the first two reference books described at the beginning of this chapter, and/or *1,818 Ways to Write Better and Get Published* by Scott Edelstein (Writer's Digest Books).

78

Legitimate Literary Agents Earn Their Money by Selling Writers' Work and Receiving a Commission (Usually 10–15 Percent)—Not Through Any Other Means.

■   ■   ■   ■   ■   ■

Standard commissions for literary agents are as follows:

Book agents: 15 percent of whatever your book earns; 20–25 percent of earnings from sales of television, film, and/or foreign rights made by the agent or their affiliate.

Television, film, and video agents: 10 percent of all earnings from any deal made by your agent; 15–20 percent on any sale of book rights to your television, film, or video made by your agent or their affiliate.

Dramatic agents: 10–15 percent of all earnings from your play (15 percent is standard); 15–20 percent for sales to stock and amateur companies; 20–25 percent for sales of television, film, or foreign rights made by the agent or their affiliate.

No agent should charge you percentages higher than these.

Furthermore, no agent should charge you a fee of *any* kind, for *any* reason, except as noted below:

- Once an agent has agreed to represent you, they may ask you to provide them with 5–15 copies of your manuscript. Others may say, "I'll just make photocopies at the copy shop down the street; I'll send you a receipt, and you can reimburse me." This is fine.

- A few agents may ask to be reimbursed for unusual (but legitimate) expenses, such as overnight delivery and overseas phone calls. There is nothing wrong with this, though it seems a bit petty to me.

- A handful of agents don't ask to be reimbursed for specific expenses, but instead ask clients to give them a small amount of money up front to cover these expenses later on. Asking for $50–$100 from clients for this purpose isn't unreasonable—but asking for more *is*.

• Instead of the usual 15 percent commission, one book agent I know charges $500 up front plus a 10 percent commission. I wouldn't accept such an arrangement *unless*: 1) the agent has already sold quite a few books; 2) they supply you with the names and phone numbers of at least two of their clients; and 3) each of those clients gives the agent a big thumbs-up.

Be very clear and careful in all your dealings with agents. In the next chapter you'll see why.

79

Many of the People Who Call Themselves Literary Agents Operate Scams and Schemes That Can Cost You Money and Do You Harm.

To become a literary agent, all you have to do is call yourself one. Unfortunately, this allows scam artists to easily set up shop and fleece writers.

Here are the most common literary scams and schemes:

- An agent tells you of the great success of their agency, then asks to see some of your work. The catch: A hefty fee is involved (perhaps $500–$1,000), but it does entitle you to a detailed written critique of your work in addition to consideration for representation. **The reality**: Your manuscript goes not to an agent, but to a flunky whose job is to write critiques. (I've seen one such critique; it was far worse than useless.) The flunky types up a letter which contains the critique, a polite turndown, and a request to see more of your work—for another fee. The crowning touch: The letter is signed by the president of the agency (who never saw your manuscript, and probably did not read the letter).

- An agent expresses interest in your work, requests it, and reads it at no charge. They respond by telling you that it has enormous promise—that it might even become a bestseller or Oscar winner—but that it needs some editing or rewriting first. It turns out that the agent can provide these very services for you, for an enormous fee—usually anywhere from $1,200 to $4,500. (Some of these scammers actually guarantee that their services will lead to publication. This is a bald-faced lie.) **The reality**: These "agents" make their living not by selling books or scripts, but by doing this overpriced editing and rewriting—which, incidentally, tends to range from second-rate to downright harmful.

- Same as above, but instead of doing the work themselves, the agent refers you to a professional editor or "book doctor," whose expertise will supposedly make the project publishable or producible. The agent adds, "Please get the project back to me as soon as the editor is done with it. I'm eager to find a home for it, and think I can do so quickly." You dutifully send your project to the editor, pay their overblown fee, obtain their services (which typically range from poor to mediocre), and then eagerly send your project back to the agent. But, alas, the agent now informs you that they're not taking on any more clients, or that the market has changed in the past few months, or that they're no longer handling your type of material. (Some scammers are bolder: One simply refuses delivery of writers' revised manuscripts.) **The reality**: These "agents" gets a kickback for each referral to the editor or book doctor. In fact, they make most or all of their money from these kickbacks, not from selling books or scripts. **Warning**: A number of bogus "publishers" operate this same scam.

- An agent agrees to read your work at no charge. After doing so, they write you a glowing letter of praise which tells you how immensely salable your project is. They then offer to represent you for a one-time fee, which can range from $400 to $1,500. You pay the fee and eagerly await the results of the agent's hard work—but you never hear from them again. They don't respond to your letters or calls, and when you do call, you always get an answering machine. **The reality**: The "agent" took your money and did nothing. **Special warning**: Some of these scammers operate "agencies" with names like Risen Christ Agency, and specialize in ripping off sincere, devout Christians.

- An agent agrees to represent your work, but charges a fee—typically $40–$75—for each submission. Although they keep trying to sell your work, they never manage to make a sale. When you call to ask about editors' or producers' responses, they say things like, "The editor at Doubleday said it's not the sort of thing they need right now" and "The people at Norton said it's not right for their company." **The reality:** This "agent" never sells anything because they are willing to "represent" anything that comes their way, no matter how awful. They do no market research and make no follow-up calls. In fact, their "representation" consists of throwing each manuscript in an envelope with a form letter, and mailing it haphazardly (but repeatedly) to a standard list of publishers and producers. (Very possibly these submissions are addressed to "Editor" or "Production Department.") These people fully expect to have everything they "represent" returned with form rejection letters, and their expectations are routinely fulfilled. Meanwhile, they take a steady stream of your money.

Sadly, most of these schemers and scammers manage to get themselves listed in one or more of the resources listed in chapter 77 (page 191–95). Usually they're kicked out by the next edition, after the complaints have started rolling in.

One last word on the subject: If you receive a printed flyer in the mail from any literary agency asking to see some of your work, there's very likely a scam or scheme behind it.

80

Don't Waste Your Time Entering Lots of Literary Contests, Particularly Those with Entry Fees.

We Americans don't want to just succeed; we want to *win*. We're not happy with coming out ahead; we want to come in *first*. Thus the huge boom in contests, literary and otherwise, in the past decade.

The problem with most literary contests—as with just about all contests—is that there can be at most a handful of winners, but there will always be a large number of losers. Your entry doesn't just have to be good—it has to be better than all (or nearly all) the others.

Compare this with the normal process of sending your work to editors or producers. If the editor of *Bicycling* likes your essay on bicycle repair for kids, there's a good chance they'll buy it and publish it. But suppose that, instead, you've entered that same piece in a feature-writing competition. Six hundred twenty people enter and the top three win cash prizes. This means your feature has to beat out at least 617 of the 620 essays for you to come away with anything at all. And because the decision will probably be made by a panel, your piece has to excite three or four different people in order to achieve anything other than failure.

Which option sounds more promising to you?

Let's compare further. If the editor at *Bicycling* likes your piece but thinks it's too similar to something the magazine published a few months back, they'll reject your piece with a polite letter asking to see more of your work. Thus the beginnings of a relationship will have been established. In contrast, if you don't win the contest, you'll get nothing but a form letter telling you that you didn't win.

Which option represents a better use of your time?

Then there is the issue of entry fees. To submit your work to an editor or producer costs nothing but postage; but to enter many contests, you may have to spend $2–$15 a pop, plus the same amount of postage. It doesn't take a rocket scientist to figure out which option is more cost-effective.

These fees are not accidents. Many literary contests exist solely or primarily to make money for their sponsors. (I've seen one competition that charges a $5 entry fee and awards a top prize of $100. The big winner in *this* contest is its organizer.)

This doesn't mean you should never enter any literary contests at all. It does mean, however, that it's wise to enter no more than a small number of contests per year. (And I would *never* send work to any magazine or book publisher that charges a reading fee simply to consider my work. This is the worst of all options: paying an entry fee without there even being a contest to win.)

Remember, no matter how talented you may be, any contest is a long shot at best. But if you write well and keep sending out your work, chances are good that positive things will happen.

Grants are another story entirely. **Grants** are sums of money given to writers (and others) for study, travel, or career development—or simply to pay their everyday expenses so they can write full-time for an extended period. Grant programs for writers are sponsored by the National Endowment for the Arts Literature Program, many state arts councils, some local and regional arts organizations, writers' centers, and private foundations such as the Guggenheim Foundation. The vast majority of these grants are for writers with at least some experience, publications, or productions under their belts. By all means apply for grants when you feel you're ready—and deserving.

For a good list of writers' grants, see the book *Grants and Awards Available for American Writers* (PEN), which is widely available in libraries, as well as by mail from PEN (568 Broadway, New York, NY 10012, 212-334-1660) for $15 postpaid.

81

Paying a "Vanity Press" to Publish Your Book Actually Discourages Bookstores from Buying It.

You've probably seen the ads in writers' magazines and the Yellow Pages that begin "Authors Wanted" or "Get Published!" or "See Your Book in Print." These are usually from **vanity presses**: publishers that will publish virtually anything that comes their way—at authors' expense.

Most vanity publishers exercise only a minimal amount of discretion. While vanity presses won't publish pornography or books advocating terrorism, they consider pretty much anything else fair game. As a result, they routinely publish vapid memoirs, collections of ninth-rate verse, and semiliterate sociopolitical ravings. Once in a while they publish something interesting as well.

Oddly enough, vanity publishers are quite honest in many ways. A vanity press will usually do exactly what it promises to do: edit your manuscript, design your book, print and bind the agreed-upon number of copies, and advertise it in its catalog. You pay for everything, of course; a typical book might cost you $10,000–$20,000 for a few thousand copies.

The big problem with vanity presses is their reputation in the marketplace. Every bookstore owner, manager, and buyer in the country knows which publishers are vanity houses—and they also know that the vast majority of their books are trash. Consequently, whenever a catalog from a vanity publisher arrives, it goes straight into the recycle bin, unopened.

This is why vanity presses sell so few copies to bookstores. Indeed, most writers who publish with vanity presses quickly discover that if they're going to sell any books at all, they have to do it themselves. Those who are not savvy about sales, promotion, and publicity usually wind up with garages full of books.

Some beginning writers mistakenly think, "Okay, so there are drawbacks. But it'll be a big break for me. I'll be published, and that will make it easier for me to be published again."

Unfortunately, precisely the opposite is true. Like bookstore owners, editors know which presses do vanity publishing. If they learn that you've published a book with a vanity house, they're not only not going to be impressed, they'll probably consider you a naive, self-indulgent rube. (So if you've *already* published a book with a vanity press, don't tell anyone in the media.)

A similar scheme goes on among songwriters who want to have their songs recorded or published. Most of these unsuspecting songwriters end up with garages full of records, tapes, or CDs.

82

Self-Publishing Is a Viable Option Only If You Know Your Market, Are Good at Promotion and Publicity, and Are Willing to Devote at Least Twenty Hours a Week to Promoting and Marketing Your Book.

■ ■ ■ ■ ■ ■ ■ ■

A far superior alternative to vanity publishing is **self-publishing**. When you publish your book yourself, you don't have to worry about the literary company you keep; you control all aspects of editing, design, printing, binding, sales, and distribution; and you get to be your book's most sincere and ardent promoter.

There's nothing shameful or second-class about self-publishing; unlike publishing with a vanity press, editors and producers won't look down on you for it. Indeed, most bookstores are perfectly willing to consider selling self-published books. Bookstore owners, managers, and buyers usually judge each self-published book on its own merits, and will take it on if they think they can sell it.

Furthermore, quite a few well-known writers have self-published their work, including Peter McWilliams, Anaïs Nin, and Herman Melville.

But self-publishing requires a substantial investment of time, money, or both to succeed. Peter McWilliams's self-published books have been very successful partly because he backed them up with a savvy and expensive marketing effort. On a smaller scale, health writer and speaker Linda Hanner successfully self-published her own first book, selling 6,000 hardcover copies in two years, by learning the ropes of public relations, becoming her own part-time publicist, appearing on dozens of talk shows, and speaking for hundreds of organizations. Linda considered her book a half-time business, and she was willing to put in twenty hours a week to promote it, publicize it, fill orders, keep accounts, and support it with her talks and media appearances.

Promotion, publicity, and marketing are usually what make

or break a book. If you're willing and able to follow Linda's or Peter's path, then self-publishing is an excellent option. On the other hand, if all of this seems daunting, then self-publishing is probably not a good idea for you.

For more information on self-publishing, consult one or more of the volumes below. (The books by Pat Bell, Peggy Glenn, Bill Henderson, John Kremer, Jeffrey Lant, and Dan Poynter are self-published.)

- *How to Get Happily Published* by Judith Appelbaum (HarperCollins)

- *Prepublishing Handbook, The* by Patricia J. Bell (Cat's-paw Press)

- *Publishing, Promoting, and Selling Your Book for Self-Publishers and Impatient Writers* by John C. Bartone (ABBE Publishers Association)

- *Publicity for Books and Authors* by Peggy Glenn (Aames-Allen Publishing)

- *Publish It Yourself Handbook, The* by Bill Henderson (Pushcart Press)

- *How to Publish, Promote, and Sell Your Own Book* by Robert L. Holt (St. Martin's Press)

- *1001 Ways to Market Your Books* by John Kremer (Open Horizons)

- *How to Make a Whole Lot More Than $1,000,000 Writing, Commissioning, Publishing, and Selling "How-To" Information* by Jeffrey Lant (JLA Publications)

- *Self-Publishing Manual, The* by Dan Poynter (Para Publishing)

- *Complete Guide to Self-Publishing, The* by Tom and Marilyn Ross (Writer's Digest Books)

83
Be Very Wary of "Copublishing" Arrangements.

■   ■   ■   ■   ■   ■   ■

Copublishing (also called **subsidy publishing**) is a hybrid of traditional book publishing and vanity publishing. In a copublishing arrangement, you and your publisher split the initial costs of designing, printing, binding, promoting, and/or publicizing your book. In exchange, you usually receive a high royalty on each copy sold—though royalties may not begin accruing until the press recoups its initial investment. Typically, you might be asked to put up about $5,000 for an initial print run of 2,000 or 3,000 copies of a five-by-eight-inch paperback.

As with both mainstream and vanity publishing, your publisher handles all the details of editing, design, printing, binding, and distribution. Usually the publisher provides some promotion and publicity, although not much. (In fact, as you'll see in a moment, you will be expected to do much of the promotion and publicity yourself.)

Unlike their counterparts at vanity presses, editors who sponsor copublishing projects tend to be pretty selective about what they publish, though somewhat less selective than editors who have to make a profit without obtaining financial assistance from their authors.

A handful of publishers, such as Griffin Publishing and Galde Press, publish primarily or exclusively under this arrangement. Also, some small and midsize presses which do standard book publishing most of the time will occasionally propose a subsidy arrangement to an author. (Usually this is when an editor thinks a book is worth publishing, but doubts it can break even under a traditional publishing setup.)

It should go without saying that there's little point in even considering subsidy publishing unless you're unable to publish your work under a traditional arrangement. So your best first step is always to make serious and sustained efforts to sign a publication contract with the likes of Houghton Mifflin, Schocken, Prima, Davies-Black, Jossey-Bass, etc.

But if it becomes clear that you've exhausted that option, should you take your book to a copublisher? Or, if you have interest from a publisher who wants to strike a copublishing deal, should you take it? Answer: maybe, but probably not.

The big plusses of copublishing are: 1) your book will compete in the marketplace on its own merits; 2) your publisher will have a decent reputation among bookstores; 3) you'll avoid the stigma of vanity publishing; and 4) the publisher's sales reps will do their best to get the book into stores.

The big minus (aside from the initial price tag) is that the typical copublished book sells only about 1,000–2,500 copies through its publisher's efforts. Selling more than 3,500 copies is quite rare—unless the author goes out and sells copies themselves.

Another big problem with copublishing is that, in some cases, it can easily become little more than vanity publishing under another name. Your copublisher may hope to sell lots of copies of its books—but if it doesn't, it has to resort to signing up more authors to make ends meet. However, because authors' financial contributions don't cover all the required costs, the copublisher has to draw in still more writers to put up even more money. As costs mount in this vicious circle, the subsidy publisher begins reneging on its obligations to some of its writers. Eventually the whole thing collapses, the publisher goes under, and lots of authors wind up with nothing at all for their investment. As I write these words, two subsidy presses (*not* the two mentioned earlier in this chapter, which seem to be healthy) have worked themselves into this vicious circle—and have generated many complaints in the process. One has been under government investigation. I do not expect either one to be around much longer.

For most writers, then, copublishing is probably a bad idea. But not for all of them. Here's the one scenario where subsidy publishing might make sense:

You have a book you'd like to see in print. That book will support your business, which involves leading workshops or giving talks on your book's subject. And whenever you give a lecture or workshop, you intend to sell copies of your book at the back of the room. You also have plans to sell the book through other means: perhaps to people on your mailing list; through ads in the newsletter you publish; through the network of professionals you're hooked into; or through a mail-order catalog business that has expressed interest in your book.

Yet, at the same time, you don't have the time, energy, or inclination to self-publish. You don't want to get involved in the details of designing, printing, or binding your book. You want individuals, businesses, and retailers to be able to order copies easily, without your having to fill the orders yourself. And you haven't had any luck with mainstream publishers—but a copublisher is seriously interested.

In your case, copublishing might not be a bad idea—*if* you genuinely feel you can sell thousands of copies of your book, either on your own or through your contacts; *if* you can work out an arrangement with the copublisher in which you can get copies of your book in bulk at very low cost; and *if* you call two of the authors the press has copublished, and both give the press good marks.

Incidentally, it's considered extremely poor form for you to approach a traditional publisher and propose a copublishing arrangement. It's even worse form to do this after the publisher has turned down your manuscript. If copublishing your book is an option, the publisher will be the one to broach the subject.

84

Avoid Sending Your Work to Poetry Anthologies That Advertise for Submissions.

■　　■　　■　　■　　■　　■

When you see a large display ad in a writers' magazine asking for poetry submissions or announcing a poetry contest, beware—there's a scheme afoot. Here's how it works (or how it would work, if you were foolish enough to fall for it):

1. The ad asks you to submit only one poem—usually of thirty lines or less. (This enables the publisher to cram poems by as many different writers as possible into one book.)

2. You send in your poem.

3. Someone reads the poem to make sure nothing in it is obscene, libelous, or illegal. If it passes this test, it's accepted for publication, along with 500–1,500 others.

4. You receive a form letter congratulating you on your artistic achievement and accepting your work for inclusion in an upcoming anthology. (If a contest is involved, you're also informed that you are now a finalist in it—i.e., yours wasn't one of the handful of rejected poems.) The letter also tells you about the beautiful hardbound volume your poem will appear in. It turns out that you won't receive any payment for your poem, or even any free copies of the anthology—but you can buy as many copies as you like at the special prepublication price of $40–$60.

5. Some months later, the book is "published"—i.e., copies are mailed to all the writers who ordered them. Otherwise, copies are pretty much unavailable. No bookstore or other retail store sells the book. The anthology receives little or no advertising, promotion, or publicity. The book probably doesn't even have a bar code or ISBN number. (Your poem appears on page 618, just

below "My Kitty, My Friend" and just above "Nazis Need Love, Too.")

6. If a contest is involved, a handful of poets in the book are identified as winners. The top two to six win cash prizes, which the publisher dutifully pays to the winning writers.

7. The publisher pockets a hefty profit—perhaps as much as $75,000.

Quite a few people currently operate such schemes. As you can see, there's nothing dishonest or illegal about them. Each publisher does everything it promises, and you're under no obligation to send them any money. (Sometimes, though, you may see in the fine print, "Anthology purchase required to ensure publication.")

But I hope you can also see that such projects are to be avoided.

Incidentally, if you get a flyer, letter, or brochure in the mail asking to see your poetry, chances are 95 percent or better that the same scheme is at work.

85

Plenty of Jobs Are Available for Writers and Editors—But They're Not Easy to Get.

■   ■   ■   ■   ■   ■

Corporations, smaller companies, nonprofits, government organizations, and of course publishers all hire full- and part-time writers and editors. Some of the positions they need to fill include:

- editors (content editors, copy editors, managing editors, acquisition editors, production editors, assistant editors, etc.)
- staff writers
- copy writers (for catalogs, instruction manuals, etc.)
- newsletter writers/editors
- technical writers/editors
- medical writers/editors
- audio/video/audiovisual/multimedia writers (particularly for business and industry)
- business writers/editors
- magazine and newspaper journalists
- TV/radio reporters
- speech writers
- public relations/public information writers
- publicists
- advertising writers
- grant writers
- ghostwriters
- researchers
- translators
- writers-in-residence
- writing instructors

- editorial assistants/editorial secretaries
- copy clerks
- proofreaders

Clearly, the good news is that there are lots of jobs for writers and editors out there. The not-so-good news is that competition is moderately to very stiff, and entry-level salaries tend to be low. (Salaries for mid- and top-level people are usually reasonable, however.)

As in most media fields, the easiest way to land one of these jobs is to know someone on the inside who can let you know of opportunities and put in a good word on your behalf. However, here are some other things that can help:

- Getting an undergraduate or (better) a graduate degree in literature, English, journalism, writing, public relations, or advertising.

- Getting some hands-on experience as a writer or editor— whether in a job, an internship, or a volunteer position.

- Publishing some of your work, preferably on a regular basis.

- Completing one of several well-known academic programs in publishing sponsored by major universities (Stanford, New York University, Harvard, and so on). For a listing of these programs, see the annual reference volume *Literary Market Place*.

86

One of the Best Ways to Land a Writing or Editing Job Is Through an Internship or Assistant's Position.

Here are the two "back doors" to getting a job as a writer or editor:

1. Become an intern. If you were to offer to work for an organization for free, purely to get some experience and industry contacts, you'd be quickly and firmly turned down. But if you were to do exactly the same thing as a student intern, there's a good chance that the response would be, "Sounds interesting. Let's talk." Here's what to do:

Make a list of half a dozen local organizations you might like to work for. Do some research in a large library to determine which departments or units in those organizations might employ writers or editors. Then call up each organization's switchboard and ask for the name of the head of each department. (Sometimes this information will turn up in your library research as well.)

Next, go to your nearest community college and enroll as a nondegree student. Sign up for one credit of internship or independent study. (It makes no difference if you're sixty years old, or if you already have a Ph.D.) The cost will probably be $60 or less.

A day or two later, call each of the department heads and say something like this: "Good afternoon. My name is _____ and I'm a student at _____. I've got a strong background in writing and editing, and I'm very interested in doing an internship with your organization, ideally in your department. Because I'm _____ years old, I've got a fair amount of real-world experience under my belt; in fact, I worked for _____ years as a _____. Would you have an interest in a student intern in the months to come, and can we meet to discuss how an internship might be set up?"

Keep trying different organizations until you get a couple of interviews. Treat these very much like job interviews: dress formally and bring a well-prepared résumé. With a little persistence and luck, you should be able to land an internship somewhere.

To complete the preliminaries, go back to the community college and find a teacher in the appropriate department to formally sponsor the internship.

Once their internships are complete, many interns are offered full- or part-time jobs at the organizations they interned for. If you work hard and prove yourself, you could become one of these people.

2. Become an assistant. If there's a particular job you'd like to have, one of the fastest ways to get it is to become the assistant of someone who has that job now.

As that person's assistant, you'll quickly get to know their job inside and out. Furthermore, once you've shown them that you're capable, you'll often be given the opportunity to take on some of their duties. Then, when they take another job, or leave the organization, or get promoted, you'll be the ideal candidate to replace them. You'll also be immensely qualified to take a similar job elsewhere.

It's not hard to get a job as an editorial secretary or assistant if you've got good word processing and organizational skills. The down side: The pay tends to be low. The up side: if you're talented, you can often move up the ladder very quickly.

Whichever strategy you use to get inside an organization, you'll probably be given mostly grunt work at first. Do it cheerfully and well, work hard, and keep your eyes and ears open.

After you've proven yourself at these tasks, offer to do some writing, editing, or other higher-level tasks for your boss. Slowly, as time passes, offer to do more and more; if appropriate, ask your boss to train you in some of their tasks or skills.

As the weeks pass, you'll get more hands-on experience and training; you'll learn about the field from the inside; you'll make important contacts; and you'll learn of potential job opportunities.

When the right one appears, go for it.

THE WRITER'S
LIFE

■ ■ ■ ■ ■ ■ ■

Building a Successful Writing Career Requires Skill, Time, Patience, Perseverance, and Flexibility. Being Good at Marketing Helps, Too.

Success comes most often—and most readily—to those who persistently work toward it.

In many ways, we writers are no different from members of any other profession. Those of us who work hard, steadily build our skills, and invest time and energy in our careers are the ones most likely to do well. Those of us who learn how to sell ourselves, our work, and our services usually do even better. And those of us who have the energy and patience to persist in the face of inevitable setbacks are the ones who tend to reap the most rewards over the long haul.

For most of us, there is no magic answer or enchanted path to follow. We should simply do our best—feeling our way one writing project, one day, and one breath at a time.

88
Your Successes and Failures As a Writer Will Be Half the Result of Your Own Effort, Half the Result of Luck.

■　　■　　■　　■　　■　　■

Just as there is no magic road to success, there are no guarantees. Working steadily toward success is important, but nothing you can do can completely ensure that success will come.

Much of what happens to us is beyond our control. All of us are subject to the influences of luck, or karma, or acts of God (take your pick). Sometimes, despite all your best efforts, a seemingly simple goal may prove utterly beyond reach. At other times, without your even trying, something wonderful may fall into your lap. None of this is unique to writers; it's how life works.

If I had to give career advice to a roomful of writers in six syllables or less, here's what I'd say: *Set goals; work hard; let go.* Decide where you want to get to; do your best to get there; but always know that the final outcome is out of your hands.

Writing Is by Nature a Solitary Activity.

But not all writers are solitary people. Some of us need to spend time with others in order to keep our sanity and emotional balance. In fact, for some of us, the more we write, the more we need to be with others.

If you are such a person, make sure you get the people contact you need. Plan time with others. Call up old friends. Reach out to acquaintances who might not feel comfortable reaching out to you. Make regular dates for fun activities with your spouse. Go square dancing. Join a book group or a bowling league. Take tango lessons.

Observe your own mind and emotions carefully, and work toward balance.

And if you're someone who prefers to be alone, that's fine, too.

Most Freelance Writers Have at Least One Other Job.

■　　■　　■　　■　　■　　■

The writing business is filled with uncertainty. Furthermore, no matter how talented you may be, or how hard you've worked to build your career, some of that uncertainty will always stay with you. It's the nature of the writing beast.

For many freelancers, particularly those with families, this uncertainty is worrisome. So we limit our risk by taking part-time jobs—as writers, editors, teachers, trainers, telephone operators, garbage collectors, or farmhands. At minimum, these jobs give us some stable income and predictable hours; at best, they help to keep our lives in balance.

I teach part-time at Hamline University, and find that the time working closely with students is the perfect complement to the time I spend alone at my computer. Other writers like to work at jobs involving movement or physical labor, which for them serves as counterpoint to the cerebral, relatively inactive task of writing.

Most freelancers, though, have some other job for a different reason: They need the money. For every freelance writer who earns their entire living from their writing, there are at least ten who have part-time jobs—and fifty who freelance part-time while holding down full-time positions.

Fortunately, freelance writing isn't an all-or-nothing profession. We can write full-time, a few hours a week, or anywhere in between. Each of us has the freedom—and the obligation—to find our own ideal balance of risk, stability, self-direction, and steady income.

91

Integrate Your Writing with the Rest of Your Life. Don't Neglect Your Family—Or Yourself—In Favor of Your Writing.

■　　■　　■　　■　　■　　■　　■

Some of the most unfortunate people I've ever met were those who tried to make writing their whole lives. Not only did their efforts do little to improve their writing, but their lives shrunk and withered.

Writing is only one part of your life. That's all it can ever be. Each of us is a human being first and a writer second.

You have relationships, obligations, and needs. Honor them. You also have insights, inspiration, and literary obsessions. Honor those, too. To the extent that you can, try not to honor any one at the expense of another.

92

When You Read Something by a Widely Published Writer and Find Yourself Saying, "I Can Write Better Than That," You're Probably Right.

■   ■   ■   ■   ■   ■

One of the paradoxes of getting published and building a writing career is that, as a beginning writer, you have to be far better than writers who have made names for themselves.

When you're first getting started, you've got no publications or other credentials to impress editors with. As a result, even before they read your work, they tend to presume that it isn't very publishable. Your writing must therefore be not merely good, but strong enough to shake editors free of their preconceptions—*and* powerful enough to overcome their fears about publishing an unknown. (From an editor's viewpoint, publishing any unknown writer presents a very real risk, in terms of both finances and reputation.)

Once you're well known, however, the situation is reversed. Because you've got abundant laurels to rest on, most editors will feel that publishing your work is an extremely safe proposition. As a result, they may cut you a good deal of slack.

Most writers have the integrity and self-respect to keep raising their standards as they become more experienced and better known. But a few get lazy. They may turn in pieces before they're really finished; they may dash off work hurriedly, just for the money; or they may even dig out things they wrote decades ago (which they couldn't sell back then) and give them to editors as "new" work.

Actually, from a historical perspective, there has never been a strict correlation between quality and publishability. While good work certainly gets published more often than bad, a significant amount of bad writing has always managed to make its way into print, and a substantial amount of very good writing never seems to get published at all. This probably hasn't changed much in the past three hundred years.

Postscript: When you read something written by a celebrity and find yourself saying, "My *thirteen-year-old* can write better than that," you're also very possibly correct. In America, celebrities are our royalty; anything they say or do, no matter how vacuous, is considered newsworthy. As a result, they are held to few of the same standards as ordinary people. (If *you* were a publisher, and Madonna's agent were to offer you her eighth-grade diary, wouldn't you publish it? And if you were Madonna, and you knew a publisher would pay you half a million dollars for your eighth-grade diary, wouldn't you sell it?)

93

It Is Up to You to Decide How Much to Network, Schmooze, and Socialize with Other Writers.

■   ■   ■   ■   ■   ■

We've all been told, "Who you know is as important as what you know and what you can do." Sadly, this is all too true. Thus the birth of networking, which has become standard practice in many circles.

Can networking help you as a writer? Yes, enormously. Can you get by without it? Yes, but your career will probably grow much more slowly.

There are two types of networking:

1. You deliberately get to know as many people who can help you as possible. If you think someone may benefit your career, you give them your business card, and thereafter send them an occasional e-mail. You attend any meeting, conference, lunch, program, or other gathering that might enhance your career or put you in touch with someone who can help you. And you always keep a positive attitude and a cheery countenance, at least when you're in public.

This is precisely the *wrong* way to go about networking.

You have another, far better option:

2. You stay open to new connections, relationships, and possibilities. You hand out your business card when the circumstances warrant or the spirit moves you. You help others with whatever information, referrals, or ideas you can reasonably provide. You're willing to ask others politely for similar assistance—though if they say no, you accept that response graciously. You attend whatever conferences, programs, or other gatherings genuinely interest you, keeping your eyes and ears open. You ask questions. When you sense a potential connection with someone, you invite that person

for tea or lunch or conversation. You stay open to what others have to say and offer.

The difference between these two types of networking is attitude. The first is based on acquisition, and it treats other human beings as stepping-stones for building a writing career. In contrast, the second is based on connection and respect for others, as well as respect for yourself.

When writers tell me they hate networking and schmoozing, it usually turns out that they hate variation 1, and they don't realize that they have another option.

With variation 2, you don't have to be someone other than yourself. You can do as much or as little networking as you feel comfortable with (though if you're a solitary type, I encourage you to push yourself somewhat). And, unlike variation 1, it becomes a natural part of your growth as a writer.

Important as networking may be, however, it should *never* become your primary task as a writer. That task is, and always will be, to write.

94

The Opinions of Any Two Writers, Editors, or Writing Teachers Will Often Differ.

Indeed, a piece you've written may generate a wide range of opinions: "I loved the first five pages, but hated the twist at the end." "The surprise ending works very well, but the buildup seems pretty pedestrian." "I saw the ending coming from page one, but otherwise I really enjoyed it; it's beautifully written."

Such differences of opinion are both common and normal—and they're just as normal for experienced writers as they are for beginners. If you were to round up thirty people at random, they're not all going to have the same opinion of Stephen King or Alice Walker or Charles Dickens.

So don't look for a consensus of opinion. You'll rarely get one.

Ultimately, *you* must be the final judge of anything you write. Only you can decide what to write and how to write it. Only you can determine how (and how much) to revise it. Only you can decide whether something you've written is finished. And only you can decide when to submit it for publication and production. As a writer, this is your most important privilege—and your most important responsibility.

95 Expect Some Negative Reviews, Reactions, and Opinions.

Once your work is published or produced, it may generate some reviews and letters. Some of these responses will be thoughtful and fair; others will be biased, vindictive, goofy, or downright addled. You may feel misjudged, maligned, or attacked. What steps should you take to defend yourself?

None. Don't bother.

Receiving some negative reviews is normal. So is receiving some stupid and unfair ones. We all get them once in a while, and there's nothing you can do to avoid them (short of ceasing to write).

What you *can* do is not take reviews seriously. If a reviewer makes some insightful comments (either positive or negative), take them to heart. But if the person's comments are way off base, just ignore them—the same way you'd ignore a street-corner prophet explaining that the world will end on Monday.

Don't bother writing a letter of rebuttal. If it's published, it may make you look petty and defensive; if it's not, you'll be even more resentful than before.

Actually, negative reviews aren't always as damaging as they may appear. For one thing, they may introduce your work to quite a few people who weren't aware of it before. For another, if your work has gotten some positive reviews as well, the primary effect of the negative ones may be to remind people that your work is out there.

When the Going Gets Tough, Reward Yourself.

As you continue to write and build your career, there will be times when things fall apart. The feature you spent six weeks researching and writing gets bumped at the last minute by an unexpected ad. Just as you're about to sign a contract for your book, the publisher calls to tell you that the company has been bought out and all projects not yet under contract have been canceled. The $4,200 check from your biggest and most reliable client bounces. After two months of laboring on it, you still can't get the ending of your new play to work. Your computer freezes up, and everything on your hard drive is lost forever. Your new poem stinks.

There will occasionally be days—and sometimes weeks or months—like this. All writers have them, even the rich and famous ones.

You can't always solve your problems or make them go away. But you *can* add good things to your life.

So, when the bad times do arrive, treat yourself well. Take yourself to a play; go for a drive in the country; have lunch at your favorite restaurant; read a book by your favorite writer; take a long hike through the woods; or just turn off the phone and do nothing for a day.

Here's a suggestion: Make a list of five things you *really* enjoy. (These should be things you can obtain reasonably easily when you want them.) Whenever bad times come, stop for a moment to catch your breath. Then pick an item from your list, get it for yourself, and enjoy it.

And don't just treat yourself well during the tough times. Reward yourself for your successes and achievements, too.

There Are Real but Limited Benefits to Joining Writers' Groups, Centers, Clubs, and Organizations.

There are literally thousands of writers' groups and organizations in North America. Most of them offer writers helpful information, classes, services, or activities. Used well and wisely, they can support your efforts to grow as a writer and build your career.

But be careful. Writers' organizations can be distracting as well as helpful. It's easy to get so involved in their activities, events, and initiatives that you don't write as much as you want or need to.

Most writers' organizations—from clubs to centers to the National Writers Union—are staffed partly or entirely by volunteers. Once you join, you'll be strongly encouraged to become one of those volunteers. And the more you get involved with the organization, the more you'll be urged to expand that involvement. Since most organizations' need for volunteers is bottomless, a vicious circle soon develops. Eventually, if you're not careful, you'll find yourself devoting way too much time to the organization, and way too little to your writing. It's particularly easy to get caught in this trap if the organization is doing good and important things.

But it's not good for you, and it's not good for your writing.

When what you give to an organization begins to exceed what you're getting out of it, stop! Look carefully at what you're doing and how it affects your writing. Then pull back as necessary—without guilt, blame, or remorse. Remember, the organization is there to serve you, not the other way around.

98

There's Something Unique to You and Your Writing That's Every Bit As Important As the Ninety-Nine Other Tips and Guidelines in This Book.

■ ■ ■ ■ ■ ■

Whatever this is, add it below. Explain or describe it in as much (or as little) detail as you like.

If you have several such items, include them all.

99

Keep Reminding Yourself Why You Write and What You Get Out of Writing.

It's easy to get blown off course in just about anything we do. The pressures of time, money, obligations, and daily life can slowly cause us to lose our way. We forget our reasons for what we do—or, worse, we start doing things that conflict with who we are and what's important to us.

If ever you find your energy or interest in writing starting to flag—or if writing is starting to become a burden instead of a joy—stop and take a step back. Reread chapter 17, and remind yourself of all the reasons why you write. Then, as quickly and steadily as you can, bring your writing back in line with your own purposes and goals as a writer.

100

Enjoy Yourself. The Very Best Reason to Write Is for the Pleasure of It.

■   ■   ■   ■   ■   ■

Whatever your reasons for writing may be, never lose sight of the most important one: sheer enjoyment.

Not coincidentally, that's also the main reason why people read.

However lofty or humble your other goals may be, if your writing can bring pleasure to you *and* to your readers, it will have made a difference in the world.

Happy writing.

Useful Resources for Writers

Except as otherwise noted, each resource listed below is available in book form. Many are also available on CD-ROM, on microfiche, and/or online.

GENERAL REFERENCE WORKS

Concise Columbia Encyclopedia, The (Houghton Mifflin/Columbia University Press). The best one-volume encyclopedia on the market.

Gregg Reference Manual, The by William A. Sabin (Glencoe/McGraw-Hill). An excellent reference book covering all the conventions of English usage.

Harbrace College Handbook by John C. Hodges (Harcourt Brace). Similar to *The Gregg Reference Manual*, but with an academic emphasis.

Random House Bad Speller's Dictionary by Joe Kay (Random House)

Poetic Meter and Poetic Form by Paul Fussell (Random House; McGraw-Hill)

Roget's 21st Century Thesaurus edited by Barbara Ann Kipfer (Dell)

World Almanac and Book of Facts (World Almanac Publications). A wonderful and concise source of general information and statistics.

OTHER GOOD BOOKS FOR BEGINNING AND INTERMEDIATE WRITERS

Bird by Bird by Anne Lamott (Pantheon; Doubleday)

No-Experience-Necessary Writer's Course, The by Scott Edelstein (Scarborough House)

1,818 Ways to Write Better and Get Published by Scott Edelstein (Writer's Digest Books)

30 Steps to Becoming a Writer—and Getting Published by Scott Edelstein (Writer's Digest Books)

Three Genres: The Writing of Poetry, Fiction, and Drama by Stephen Minot (Prentice Hall)

Writing Down the Bones by Natalie Goldberg (Shambhala)

MANUSCRIPT FORM

Writer's Digest Guide to Manuscript Formats, The by Dian Dincin Buchman and Seli Groves (Writer's Digest Books)

SOURCES OF INFORMATION ON EDITORS, PRODUCERS, PUBLISHERS, THEATERS, AND PRODUCTION COMPANIES

Bacon's Magazine Directory (reference book, published annually). Lists many of the magazines published in North America, along with editors' names, positions, addresses, and phone numbers.

Bacon's Newspaper Directory (reference book, published annually). Provides a good list of newspapers of all sizes throughout North America, along with addresses, phone numbers, and editors' names.

Canadian Writer's Guide (reference book, published every other year). A good general reference covering Canadian markets.

Canadian Writer's Market (reference book, published annually). A guide to a wide range of Canadian markets for writers.

Children's Writer's and Illustrator's Market (reference book, published annually). A useful guide to a wide range of children's markets.

Directory of Literary Magazines (reference book, published annually). Quite helpful for poets and writers of literary fiction.

Dramatists Sourcebook (reference book, published annually). Probably the best market guide for playwrights.

Editor and Publisher International Year Book (reference book, published annually). A useful list of newspapers throughout North America and elsewhere, with addresses, phone numbers, and editors' names.

Freelance Writer's Report (newsletter, published monthly). CNW Publishing, Box A, North Stratford, NH 03590, 800-351-9278. A good source of general market information.

Hollywood Creative Directory (reference book, published each March, July, and November). A first-rate guide to Hollywood studios, production companies, and TV networks. The single best resource for writers of material for film and television.

Independent Publisher (magazine, published every other month). The Jenkins Group, 121 East Front Street, Suite 401, Traverse City, MI 49684, 616-933-0445. A good source of information on what many small- and medium-sized book publishers are publishing. The spring and fall "announcements" issues are especially useful.

International Directory of Little Magazines and Small Presses (reference book, published annually). Provides information on a wide variety of literary magazines and book publishers.

International Literary Market Place (reference book, published annually). A helpful list of book publishers outside of North America.

Library Journal (magazine, published once or twice a month, depending on the month). Cahners, 245 West 17th Street, New York, NY 10011, 800-523-9659. Through its articles, reviews, and ads, *LJ* provides a great deal of information on what hundreds of different book publishers are publishing. The spring, summer, and fall "new books" issues are especially helpful.

Literary Market Place (reference book, published annually). An excellent guide for writers hoping to publish their books. Contains information on a wide range of American and Canadian publishers, as well as book producers, literary agents, and other book publishing organizations and professionals.

Member List. Alliance of Resident Theatres/New York, 575 Eighth

Avenue, Suite 175, New York, NY 10018, 212-989-5257. A listing of markets for plays in New York City.

New Media Directory (reference book, published annually). A useful directory of online and other new media markets.

Newsletters in Print (reference book, published every other year). An excellent source of information on a wide variety of newsletter markets.

Novel and Short Story Writer's Market (reference book, published annually). A useful and wide-ranging guide to markets for fiction.

Oxbridge Directory of Newsletters (reference book, published annually). A very good list of U.S. and Canadian newsletter markets.

Poet's Market (reference book, published annually). An excellent resource for poets looking to publish their work; covers both magazine and book publishers.

Poets & Writers (magazine, published every other month). Poets & Writers, 72 Spring Street, Suite 301, New York, NY 10012, 212-226-3586. Provides information on a wide variety of markets, but is particularly strong on literary magazines and literary presses.

Publishers Directory (reference book, published annually). A useful list of many book publishers, especially small, noncommercial ones.

Publishers Trade List Annual (reference book, published annually). An anthology of catalogs from a wide range of book publishers. Helpful for writers looking to publish their books.

Publishers Weekly (magazine, published weekly). Cahners, 245 West 17th Street, New York, NY 10011, 800-278-2991. This is the trade journal of the book publishing industry, and, thus, one of the best resources for writers seeking publishers for their books. The articles, reviews, and ads all provide lots of useful information. Particularly helpful are the spring, summer, and fall "announcements" issues, as well as the special issues highlighting children's books, religious books, business books, and other specialized areas of book publishing.

School Library Journal (magazine, published monthly). Cahners,

245 West 17th Street, New York, NY 10011, 800-456-9409. Through articles, reviews, and ads, *SLJ* provides helpful information on presses that publish books for children and young adults.

Small Press Review (magazine, published monthly). Provides a helpful look at what a variety of literary presses are publishing.

Songwriter's Market (reference book, published annually). The single best reference for songwriters.

Syndicate Directory (reference book, published every other year). A guide to newspaper and magazine syndicates that distribute columns and comics.

Theatre Directory (reference book, published annually). A useful list of markets for playwrights.

Theatre Profiles (reference book, published every other year). Theatre Communications Group, 255 Lexington Avenue, New York, NY 10017, 212-697-5230. Lists all the productions during the current or previous year for hundreds of theaters around the United States.

Working Press of the Nation, The (reference book, published annually). Volume 1 provides a thorough list of newspapers throughout the United States, along with addresses, phone numbers, and editors' names. Volume 2 provides a similar list for magazines.

Writer's Chronicle, The (magazine, published six times a year). Associate Writing Programs, George Mason University, Tallwood House, Mail Stop 1E3, Fairfax, VA 22030, 703-993-4301. A good source of information on literary magazines and presses.

Writer's Digest (magazine, published monthly). By far the best magazine for writers, and a helpful source of general (though not extensive) market information.

Writer's Guide to Book Editors, Publishers, and Literary Agents (reference book, published annually). The single best source of information on book publishers and the editors who work for them. Contains special sections on religious/spiritual and university presses. An invaluable resource for anyone who hopes to publish a book.

Writer's Market (reference book, published annually). A very large, and very informative, guide to markets of many different types, including book publishers (both North American and foreign), book producers, magazines, theaters, newspaper syndicates, film and TV producers, and greeting card publishers. Contains an excellent list of trade, technical, and professional journals.

CONTRACT NEGOTIATION FOR WRITERS

Indispensable Writer's Guide, The by Scott Edelstein (Harper-Collins)
Negotiating a Book Contract by Mark L. Levine (Moyer Bell)
1,818 Ways to Write Better and Get Published by Scott Edelstein (Writer's Digest Books)
Writer's Guide to Contract Negotiation, A by Richard Balkin (Writer's Digest Books)

PREPARING A BOOK PROPOSAL

Nonfiction

How to Write a Book Proposal by Michael Larsen (Writer's Digest Books)
1,818 Ways to Write Better and Get Published by Scott Edelstein (Writer's Digest Books)
Write the Perfect Book Proposal: 10 That Sold and Why by Jeff Herman and Deborah Adams (Wiley)

Fiction

Manuscript Submission by Scott Edelstein (Writer's Digest Books)

LITERARY AGENTS

Guide to Literary Agents edited by Donya Dickerson (Writer's Digest Books). Published annually in January.

Hollywood Agents and Managers Directory (HCD). Published each February and October. Contains a good list of agents who represent material for film and TV.

Literary Market Place (Reed Elsevier). Published annually in October.

National Writers Union, The (113 University Place, 6th Floor, New York, NY 10003, 212-254-0279) maintains an online database of book agents which is based on an annual survey of its members. Available only to NWU members, though virtually all writers may join.

Writer's Guide to Book Editors, Publishers, and Literary Agents by Jeff Herman (Prima). Published annually in September (the 2000-01 edition will be published in late 1999).

WRITING FOR BUSINESSES AND NONPROFITS

Secrets of a Freelance Writer by Robert W. Bly (Henry Holt)

Writing for the Corporate Market by George Sorenson (Mid-List Press)

REGISTRATION SERVICES FOR TV AND FILM SCRIPTS
In the United States

Writers Guild West, The, 7000 West 3rd Street, Los Angeles, CA 90048, 213-951-4000; or The Writers Guild East, 555 West 57th Street, Suite 1230, New York, NY 10019, 212-757-4360.

In Canada

Writers Guild of Canada, The, 123 Edward Street, Suite 1225, Toronto, ON M5G 1EZ, 416-979-7907.

GRANTS AND AWARDS FOR WRITERS

Grants and Awards Available for American Writers (PEN, 568 Broadway, New York, NY 10012, 212-334-1660). $15 postpaid.

SELF-PUBLISHING

Complete Guide to Self-Publishing, The by Tom and Marilyn Ross (Writer's Digest Books)

How to Get Happily Published by Judith Appelbaum (Harper-Collins)

How to Make a Whole Lot More Than $1,000,000 Writing, Commissioning, Publishing and Selling "How-To" Information by Jeffrey Lant (JLA Publications)

How to Publish, Promote, and Sell Your Own Book by Robert L. Holt (St. Martin's Press)

1001 Ways to Market Your Books by John Kremer (Open Horizons)

Prepublishing Handbook, The by Patricia J. Bell (Cat's-paw Press)

Publicity for Books and Authors by Peggy Glenn (Aames-Allen Publishing)

Publishing, Promoting, and Selling Your Book for Self-Publishers and Impatient Writers by John C. Bartone (ABBE Publishers Association)

Publish It Yourself Handbook, The by Bill Henderson (Pushcart Press)

Self-Publishing Manual, The by Dan Poynter (Para Publishing)

COURSES AND PROGRAMS IN PUBLISHING

Literary Market Place (Reed Elsevier). Annual reference book, published each October; available in many large libraries.

WRITERS' RESOURCES ON THE WEB
(compiled by Tess Meara exclusively for this book)

Market Listings

http://www.inkspot.com/classifieds/

A large and varied listing of markets for writers, updated daily.

http://www.writersdigest.com/guidelines/index.htm

Allows you to search *Writer's Digest* updates online. http://

www.awoc.com/Guidelines.cfm
> Searchable database of 600+ markets.

http://www.awoc.com/WFD.cfm
> Subscription link for *Writing for Dollars,* a free markets newsletter.

http://www.pw.org/mag/
> Web site for *Poets & Writers* magazine. Includes an excellent guide to literary markets and grants for writers.

http://www.webwitch.com/writers/markets.html *and*
http://www.webwitch.com/writers/markets.html#ezines
> Listings of online markets for writers, including small press markets.

Writing for New Media

Silicon Alley Reporter
> http://www.siliconalleyreporter.com/

World Wide Web Artists Consortium
> http://wwwac.org/

http://www.communicator.com/
> Excellent resource and links page for film, TV, and new media writers.

General Information and Resources for Writers

http://members.xoom.com/GilaQueen/hotlinks.htm
> Links to writers' organizations in many fields.

http://webreference.com/internet/magazines/
> A reference for both computer-geek and business-type web publications. Whether you program, sell widgets on the web, or use the web for research, you may find something of interest here.

http://www.bookwire.com/
> News and information on the book publishing world.

http://www.ecola.com/
> Online "newsstand" with links to online newspapers, magazines, and other publications.

http://www.edoc.com/ejournal/magazines.html
   A large listing of online journals.
http://www.meer.net/~johnl/e-zine-list/index.html
   A huge list of e-zines, sorted by eighty keywords and by title.
   Some of these are paying markets, some are not.
http://www.vcu.edu/artweb/playwriting/dg.html
   A very highly regarded resource for playwrights.
http://www.yahoo.com/Social_Science/Communications/Writing/
   Yahoo's resource page for writers.

Major Writers Organizations: United States

The American Academy of Poets
   http://www.poets.org/
American Society of Journalists and Authors
   http://www.asja.org/
Associated Writing Programs
   http://www.gmu.edu/depts/awp/
   This organization is for writers of serious fiction, nonfiction,
   and poetry, as well as people who teach creative writing on
   the college level.
The Authors Guild
   http://www.authorsguild.org/
Mystery Writers of America
   http://www.mysterynet.com/mwa/
National Writers Union
   http://www.nwu.org/
PEN
   http://pen.org/
Poetry Society of America
   http://www.poetrysociety.org/
Romance Writers of America
   http://www.rwanational.com/
Science Fiction Writers of America
   http://www.sfwa.org/
   This site's links page provides excellent market information.
Society of Children's Book Writers and Illustrators
   http://www.scbwi.org/

Society for Technical Communication
   http://stc.org/
   This is the professional organization of technical writers.
Writers Guild of America
   http://www.wga.org/
   WGA is the organization of professional American screen-writers.

Major Writers Organizations: Canada

Canadian Authors Association
   http://www.canauthors.org/national.html
The Writers' Union of Canada
   http://www.swifty.com/twuc/
Periodical Writers Association of Canada
   http://www.web.net/~pwac/

Scott Edelstein is best known for his highly popular books which inform and empower writers. These include *30 Steps to Becoming a Writer—and Getting Published* (Writer's Digest Books), *1,818 Ways to Write Better and Get Published* (Writer's Digest Books), *The No-Experience-Necessary Writer's Course* (Scarborough House), and *Manuscript Submission* (Writer's Digest Books).

He has also published ten other books on a variety of subjects, from college success to life insurance to the future of entertainment. In addition, well over 100 of his short stories and articles have appeared in magazines and anthologies around the world.

Over the past twenty years, Scott has worked as a book, magazine, and newspaper editor; a literary agent; a magazine and newspaper journalist; a writing and publishing consultant; a freelance writer, editor, and ghostwriter; a magazine columnist; an arts reviewer; a manuscript critic; a writer of material for businesses and nonprofits; and a teacher at many colleges and universities. He frequently gives talks and workshops for writers at universities and writers' centers, and works one on one with writers to help them publish their work and build their writing careers. He currently teaches writing at Hamline University in St. Paul, Minnesota.

Scott lives with his wife and stepdaughter (also a writer) in Minneapolis, where he continues to write, edit, and consult.